SUPER EASY SONGBOOK

BROADWAY

ISBN 978-1-4950-7254-3

7777 W. BLUEMOUND RD. P.O. BOX 13819 MILWAUKEE, WI 53213

Visit Hal Leonard Online at
www.halleonard.com

Welcome to the *Super Easy Songbook* series!

This unique collection will help you play your favorite songs quickly and easily. Here's how it works:

- Play the simplified melody with your right hand. Letter names appear inside each note to assist you.

- There are no key signatures to worry about! If a sharp ♯ or flat ♭ is needed, it is shown beside the note each time.

- There are no page turns, so your hands never have to leave the keyboard.

- If two notes are connected by a tie ⌣, hold the first note for the combined number of beats. (The second note does not show a letter name since it is not re-struck.)

- Add basic chords with your left hand using the provided keyboard diagrams. Chord voicings have been carefully chosen to minimize hand movement.

- The left-hand rhythm is up to you, and chord notes can be played together or separately. Be creative!

- If the chords sound muddy, move your left hand an octave* higher. If this gets in the way of playing the melody, move your right hand an octave higher as well.

  * *An octave spans eight notes. If your starting note is C, the next C to the right is an octave higher.*

—————————————————— ALSO AVAILABLE ——————————————————

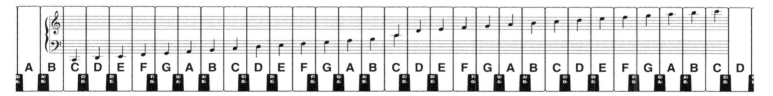

Hal Leonard Student Keyboard Guide HL00296039

Key Stickers HL00100016

All I Ask of You
from THE PHANTOM OF THE OPERA

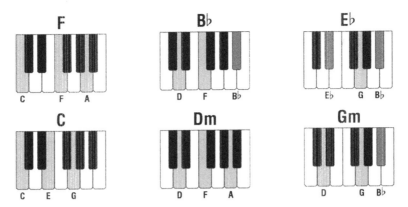

Music by Andrew Lloyd Webber
Lyrics by Charles Hart
Additional Lyrics by Richard Stilgoe

Quietly, with emotion

No more talk of dark - ness, for - get these wide - eyed fears. I'm

here, noth - ing can harm you, my words will warm and calm you.

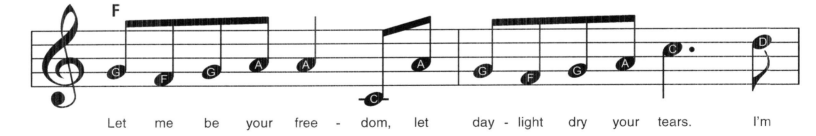

Let me be your free - dom, let day - light dry your tears. I'm

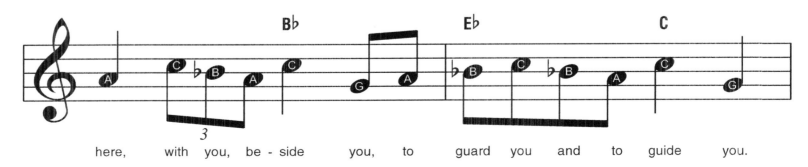

here, with you, be - side you, to guard you and to guide you.

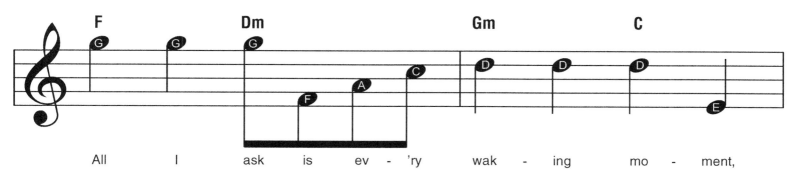

All I ask is ev - 'ry wak - ing mo - ment,

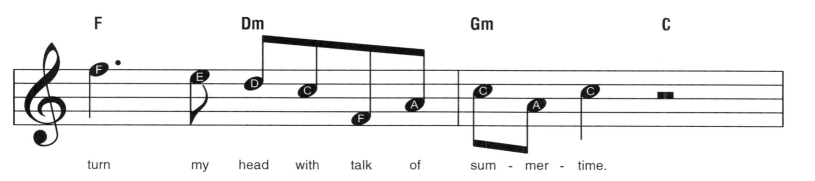

turn my head with talk of sum - mer - time.

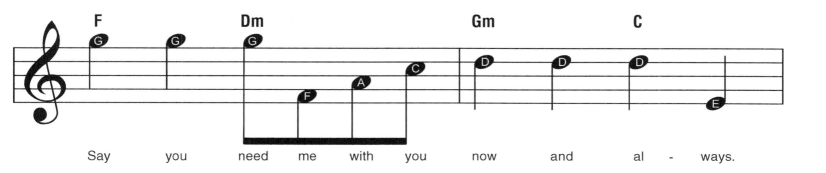

Say you need me with you now and al - ways.

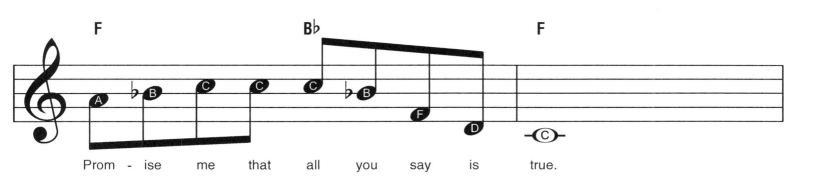

Prom - ise me that all you say is true.

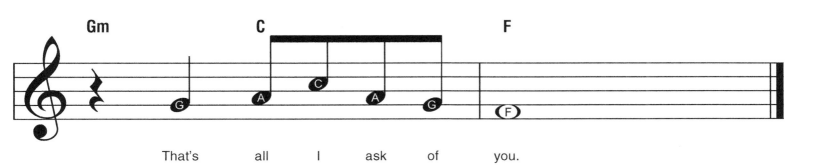

That's all I ask of you.

Baubles, Bangles and Beads

from KISMET

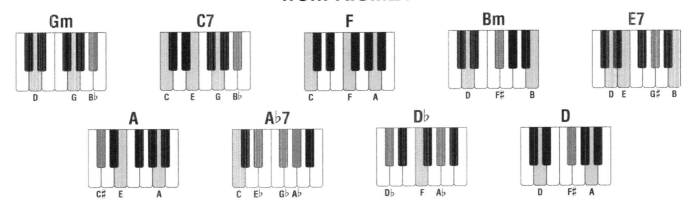

Words and Music by Robert Wright
and George Forrest
(Music Based on Themes of A. Borodin)

Moderate Waltz

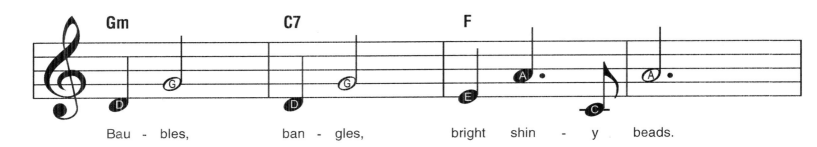

Bau - bles, ban - gles, hear how they jing, jing - a - ling - a.

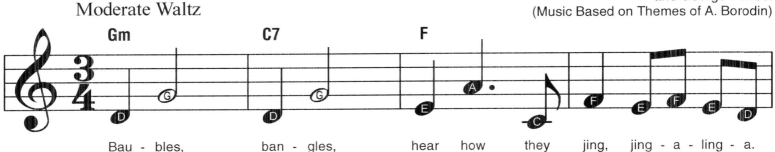

Bau - bles, ban - gles, bright shin - y beads.

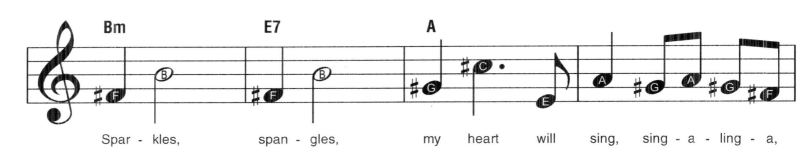

Spar - kles, span - gles, my heart will sing, sing - a - ling - a,

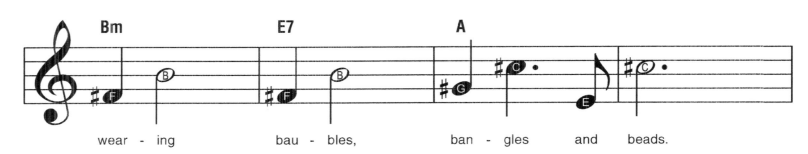

wear - ing bau - bles, ban - gles and beads.

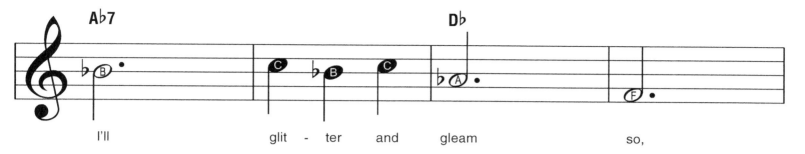

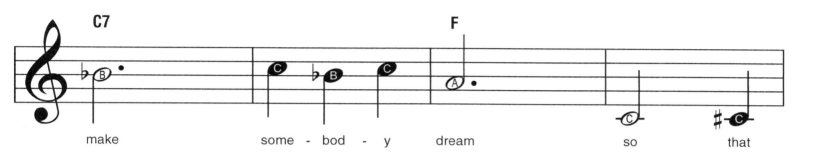

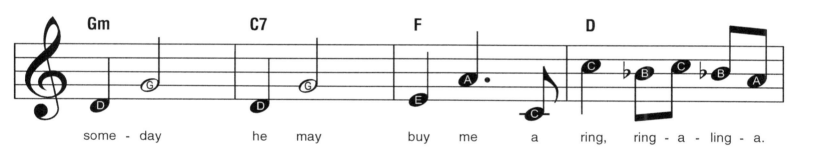

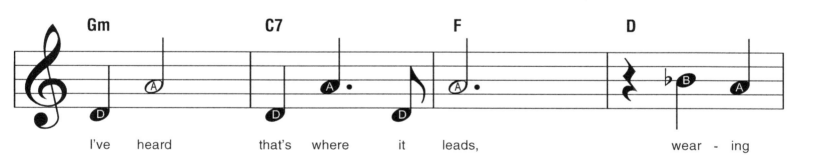

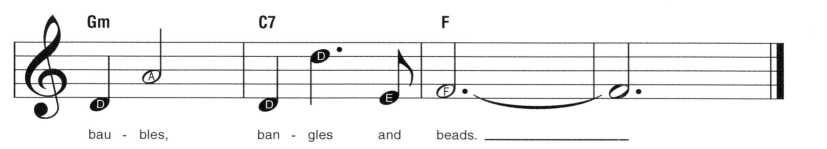

Blue Skies

from BETSY

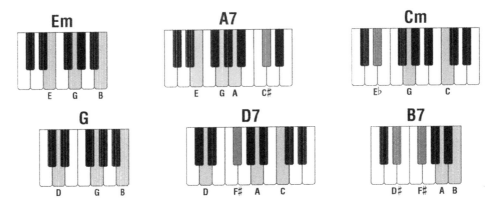

Words and Music by
Irving Berlin

Moderately

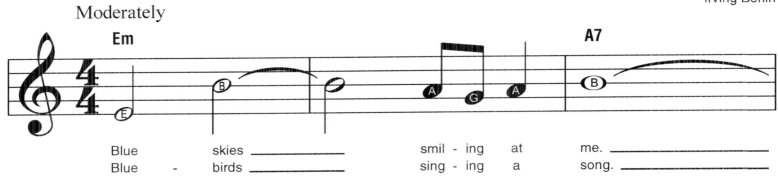

Blue   skies _____ smil - ing   at   me. _____
Blue - birds _____ sing - ing   a   song. _____

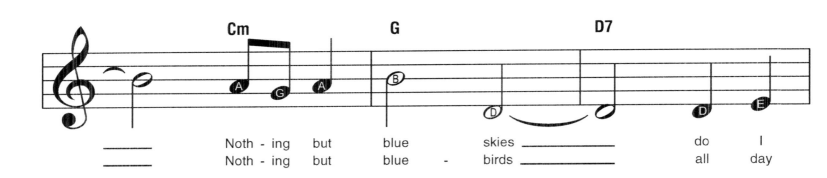

_____ Noth - ing   but   blue   skies _____ do   I
_____ Noth - ing   but   blue - birds _____ all   day

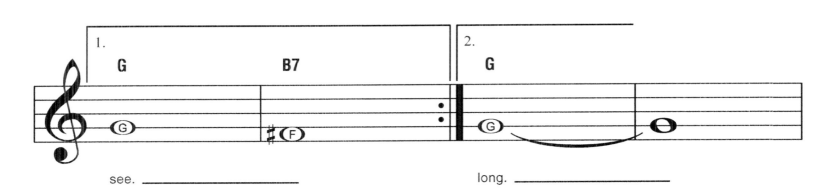

see. _____   long. _____

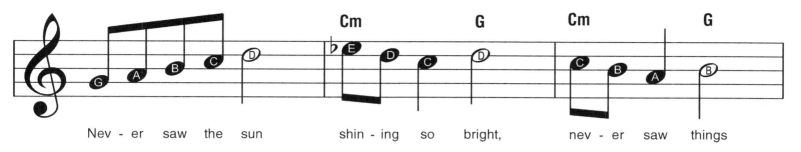

Nev - er saw the sun shin - ing so bright, nev - er saw things

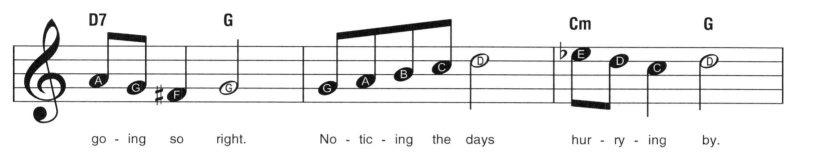

go - ing so right. No - tic - ing the days hur - ry - ing by.

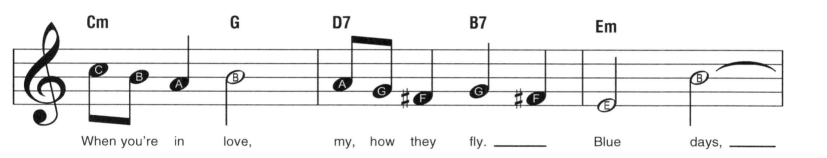

When you're in love, my, how they fly. _____ Blue days, _____

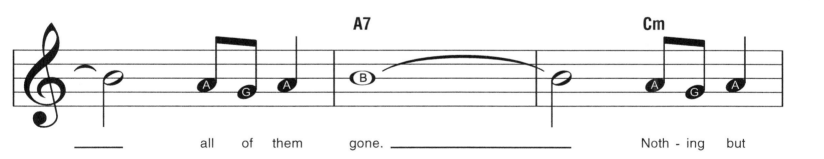

_____ all of them gone. _____ Noth - ing but

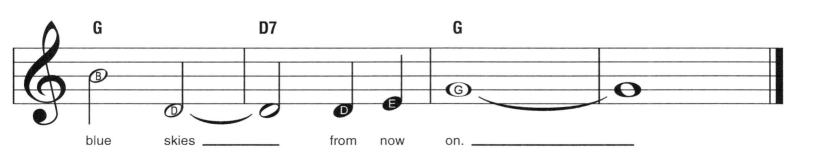

blue skies _____ from now on. _____

Bring Him Home
from LES MISÉRABLES

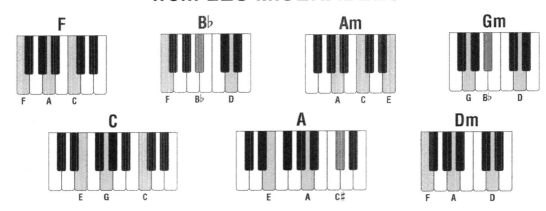

Music by Claude-Michel Schönberg
Lyrics by Herbert Kretzmer and Alain Boublil

With much expression

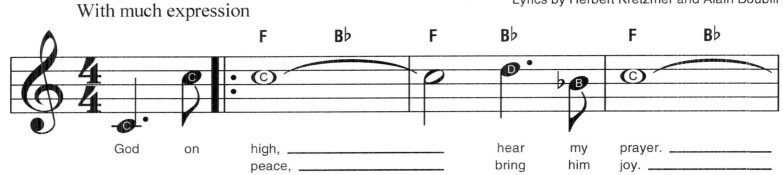

God   on   high, _____   hear   my   prayer. _____
peace, _____   bring   him   joy. _____

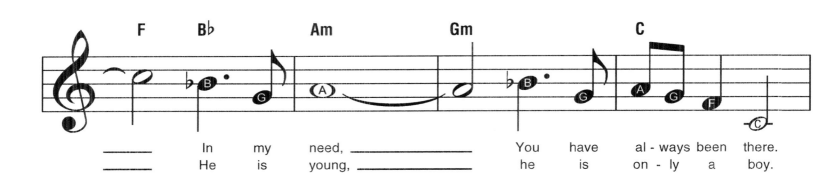

_____   In   my   need, _____   You   have   al - ways   been   there.
_____   He   is   young, _____   he   is   on - ly   a   boy.

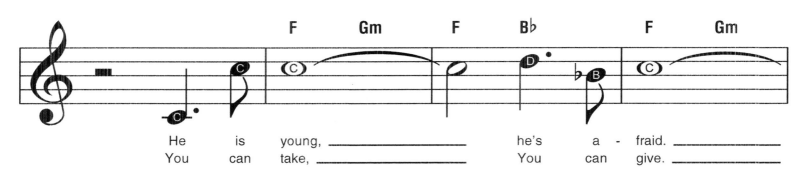

He   is   young, _____   he's   a - fraid. _____
You   can   take, _____   You   can   give. _____

13

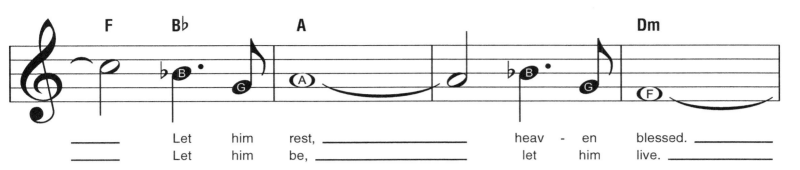

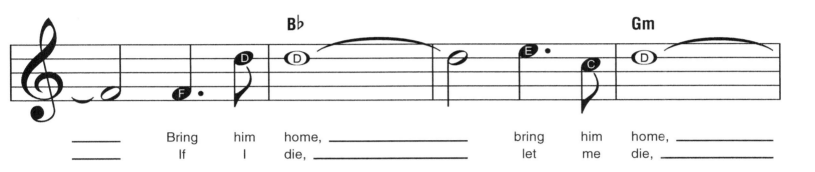

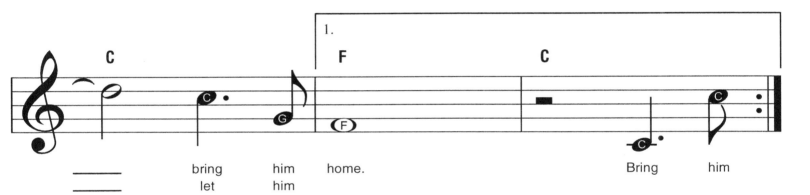

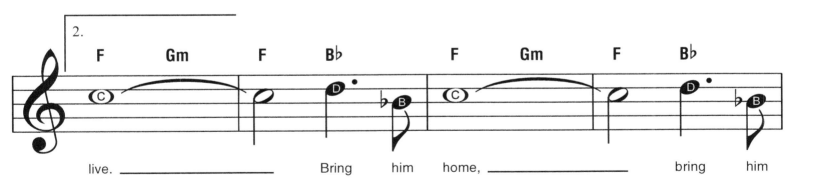

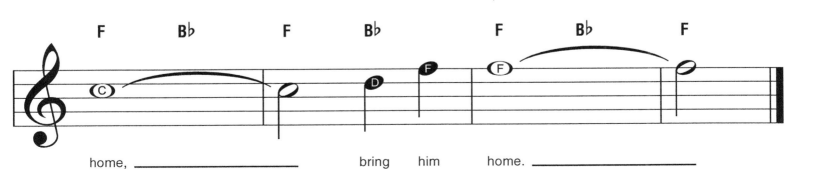

Cabaret
from the Musical CABARET

Words by Fred Ebb
Music by John Kander

Can You Feel the Love Tonight

from THE LION KING: THE BROADWAY MUSICAL

Music by Elton John
Lyrics by Tim Rice

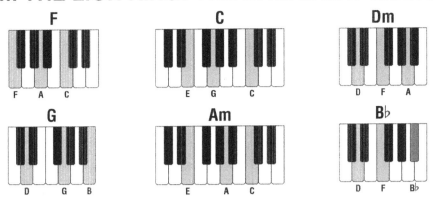

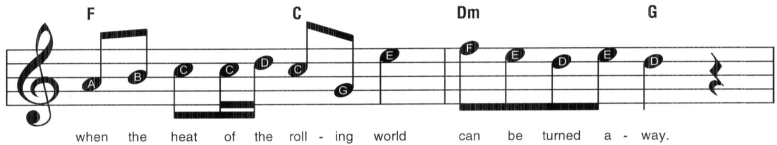

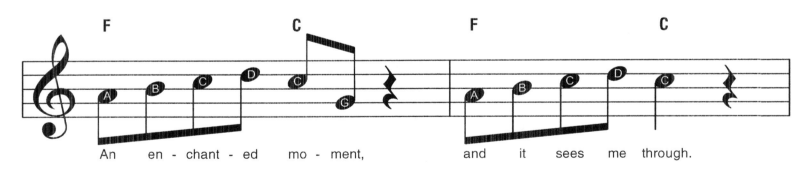

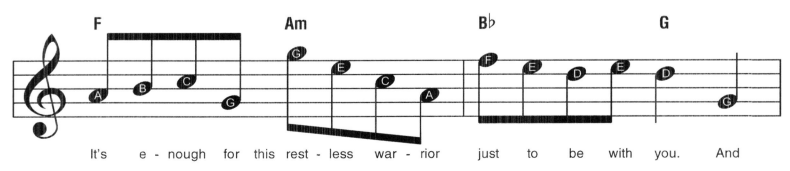

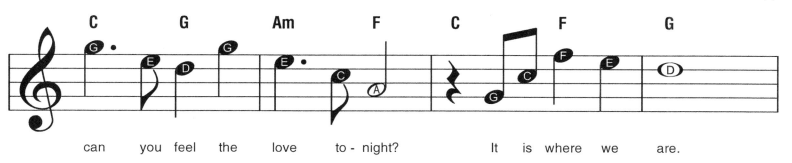

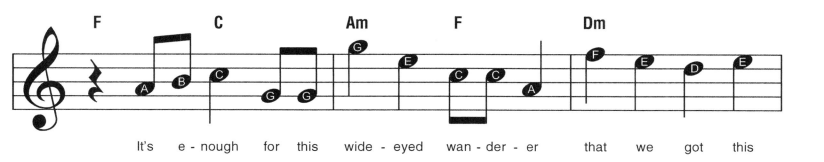

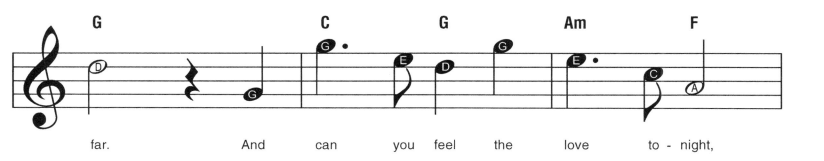

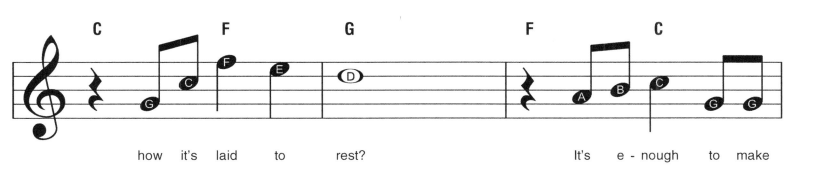

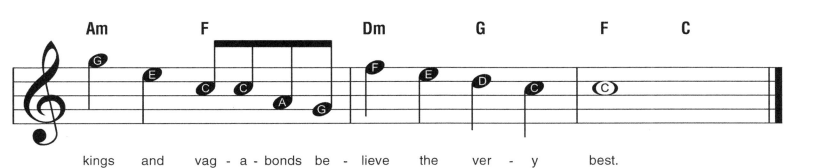

Can't Help Lovin' Dat Man

from SHOW BOAT

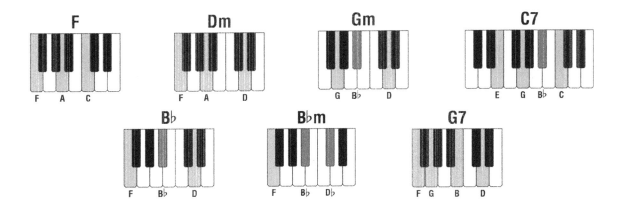

Lyrics by Oscar Hammerstein II
Music by Jerome Kern

Moderate Shuffle

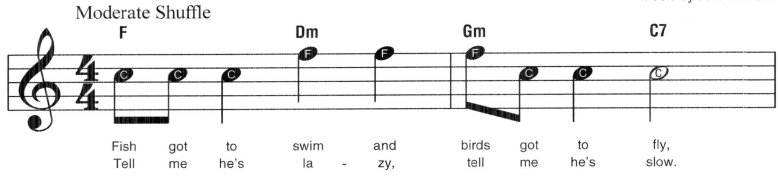

Fish got to swim and birds got to fly,
Tell me he's la - zy, tell me he's slow.

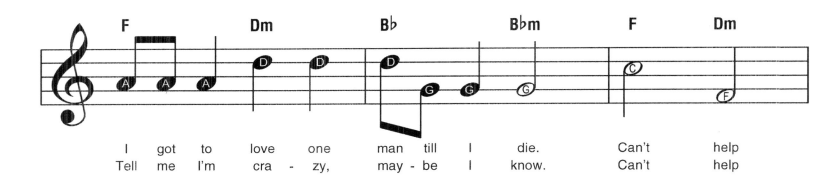

I got to love one man till I die. Can't help
Tell me I'm cra - zy, may - be I know. Can't help

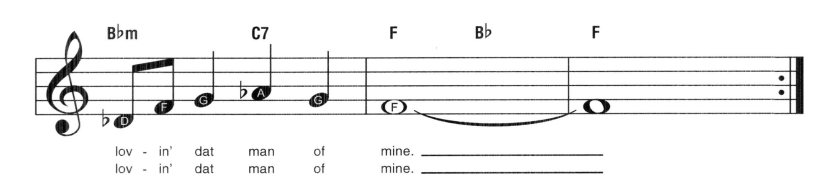

lov - in' dat man of mine.
lov - in' dat man of mine.

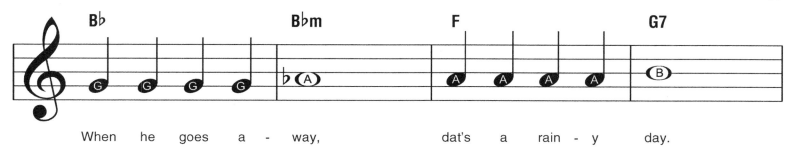

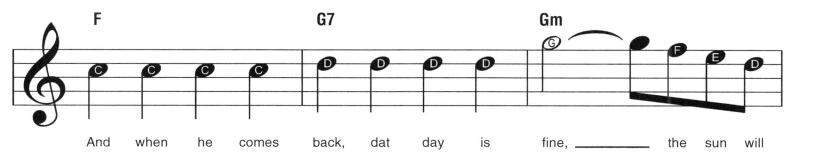

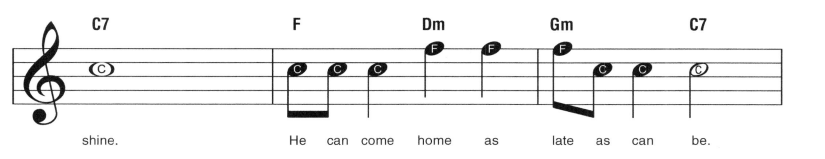

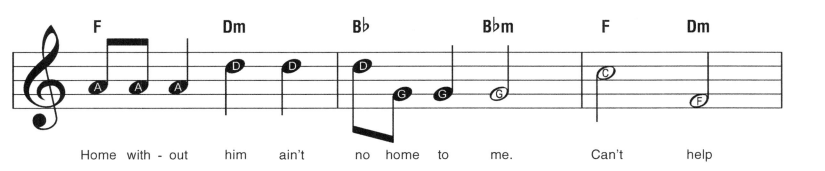

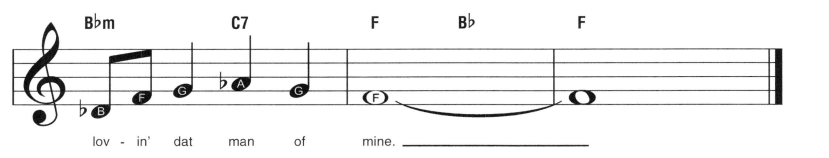

Close Every Door
from JOSEPH AND THE AMAZING TECHNICOLOR® DREAMCOAT

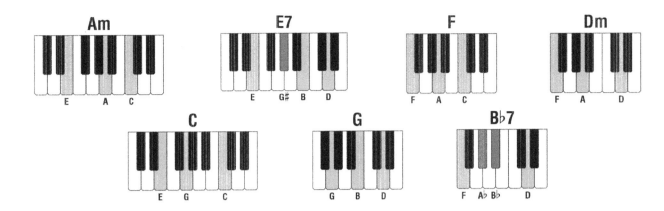

Music by Andrew Lloyd Webber
Lyrics by Tim Rice

Moderately

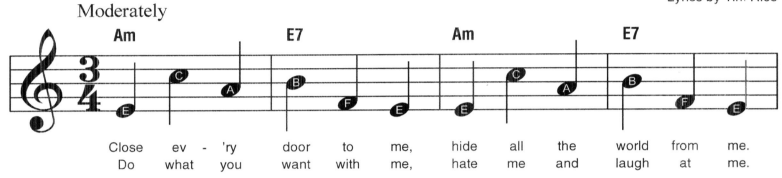

Close ev - 'ry door to me, hide all the world from me.
Do what you want with me, hate me and laugh at me.

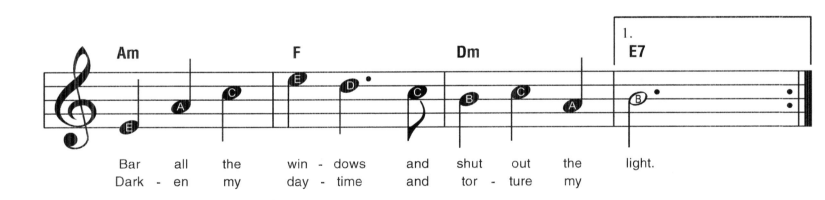

Bar all the win - dows and shut out the light.
Dark - en my day - time and tor - ture my

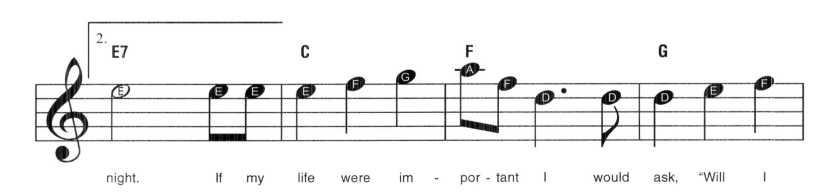

night. If my life were im - por - tant I would ask, "Will I

21

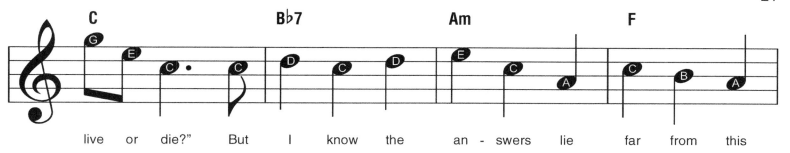

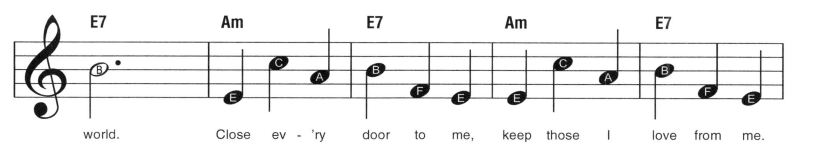

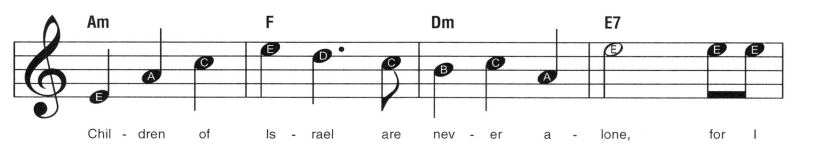

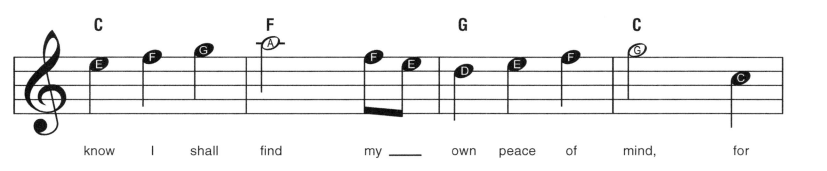

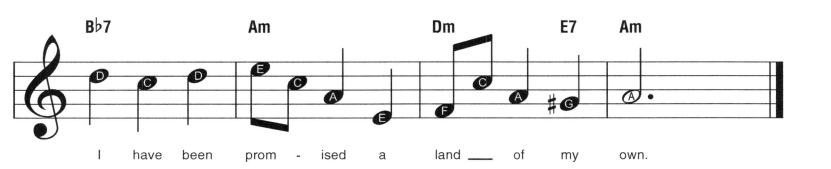

Comedy Tonight
from A FUNNY THING HAPPENED ON THE WAY TO THE FORUM

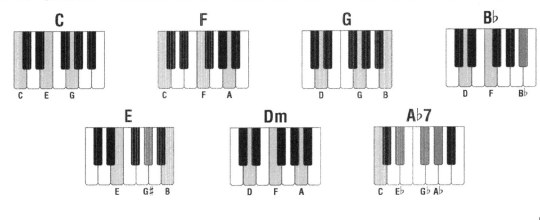

Music and Lyrics by
Stephen Sondheim

Lively

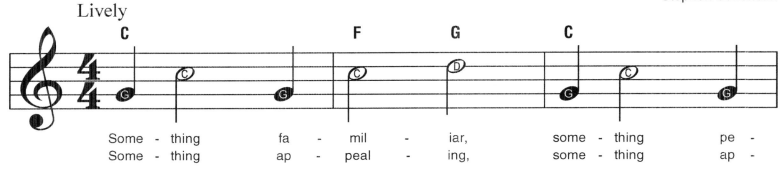

Some - thing fa - mil - iar, some - thing pe -
Some - thing ap - peal - ing, some - thing ap -

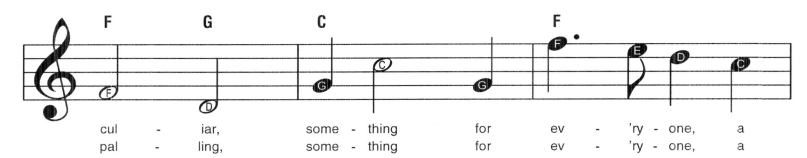

cul - iar, some - thing for ev - 'ry - one, a
pal - ling, some - thing for ev - 'ry - one, a

com - e - dy to - night!
com - e - dy to - night! Noth - ing with

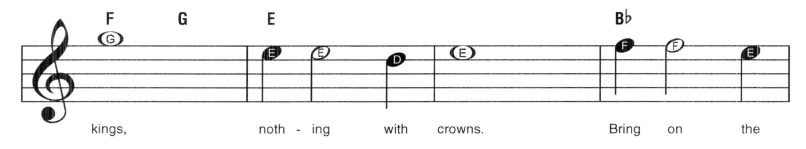

kings, noth - ing with crowns. Bring on the

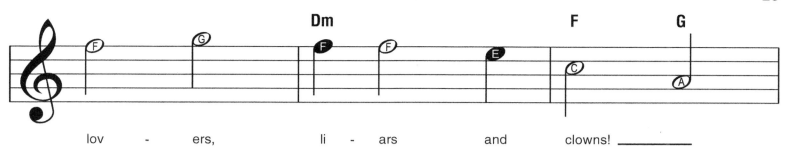

lov - ers, li - ars and clowns! _____

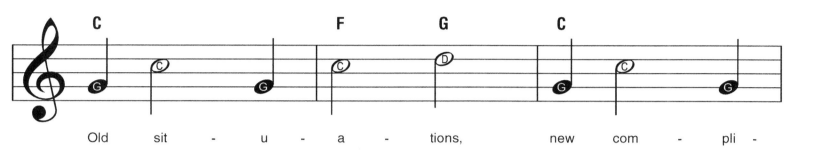

Old sit - u - a - tions, new com - pli -

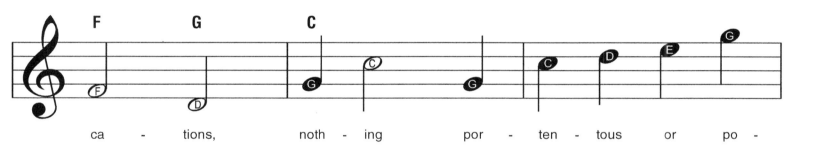

ca - tions, noth - ing por - ten - tous or po -

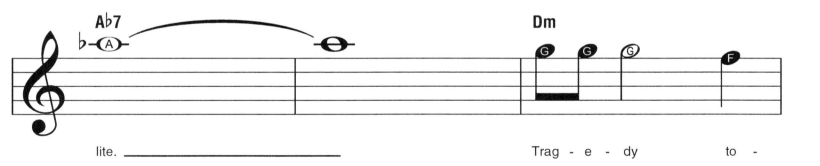

lite. _____ Trag - e - dy to -

mor - row, com - e - dy to - night!

Dancing Queen

from MAMMA MIA!

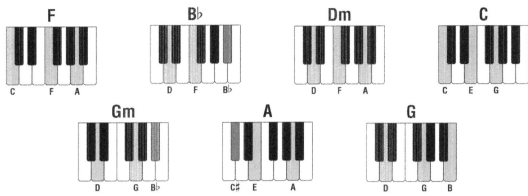

Words and Music by Benny Andersson,
Björn Ulvaeus and Stig Anderson

25

Day by Day
from the Musical GODSPELL

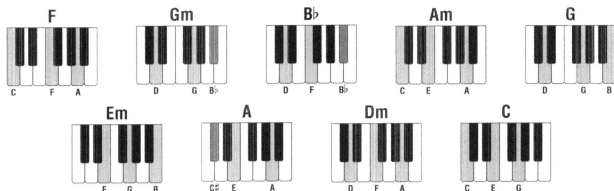

Music and New Lyrics by
Stephen Schwartz
Original Lyrics by
Richard of Chichester (1197-1253)

Let the Sunshine In

from the Broadway Musical Production HAIR

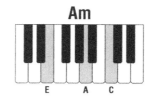

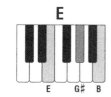

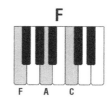

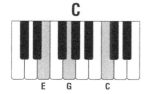

Words by James Rado
and Gerome Ragni
Music by Galt MacDermot

Happy Pop feel

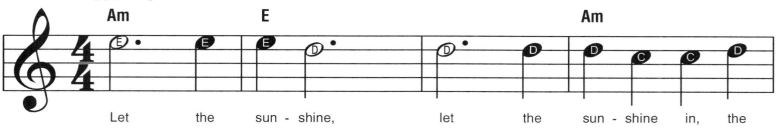

Let the sun - shine, let the sun - shine in, the

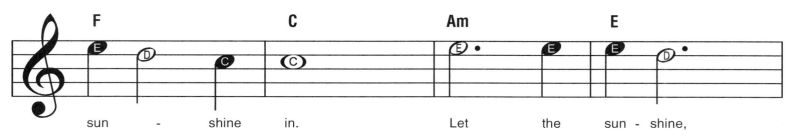

sun - shine in. Let the sun - shine,

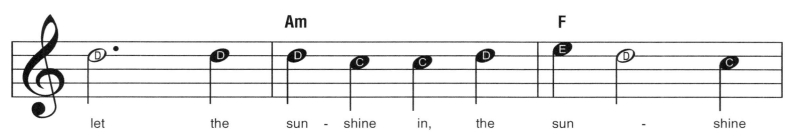

let the sun - shine in, the sun - shine

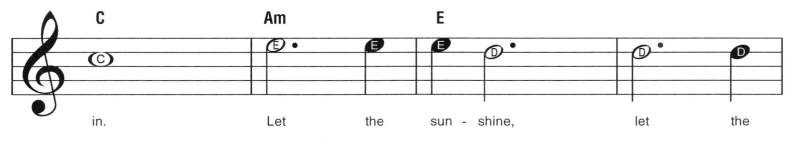

in. Let the sun - shine, let the

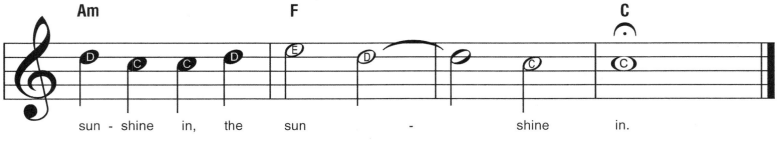

sun - shine in, the sun - shine in.

Defying Gravity
from the Broadway Musical WICKED

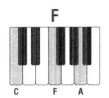
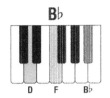
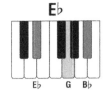
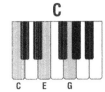
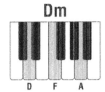

Music and Lyrics by
Stephen Schwartz

With energy

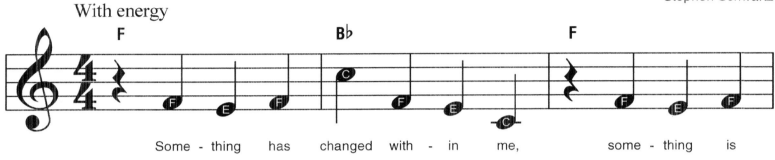

Some - thing has changed with - in me, some - thing is

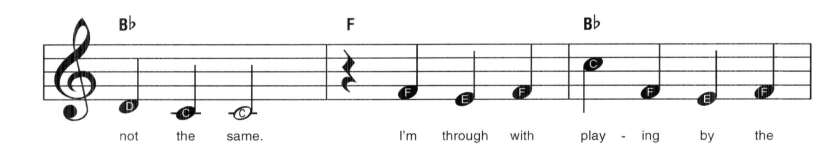

not the same. I'm through with play - ing by the

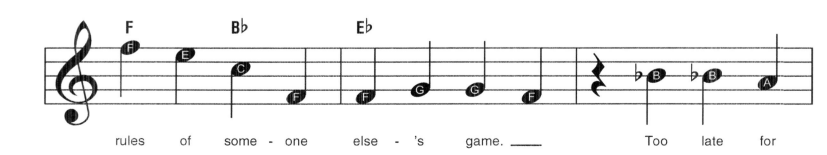

rules of some - one else - 's game. _____ Too late for

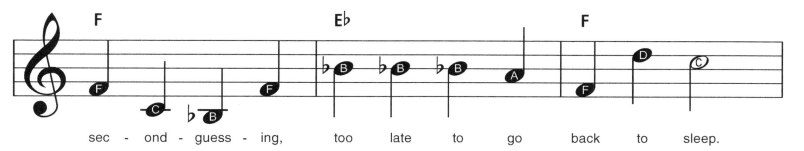

sec - ond - guess - ing, too late to go back to sleep.

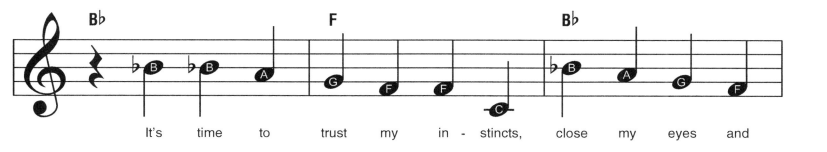

It's time to trust my in - stincts, close my eyes and

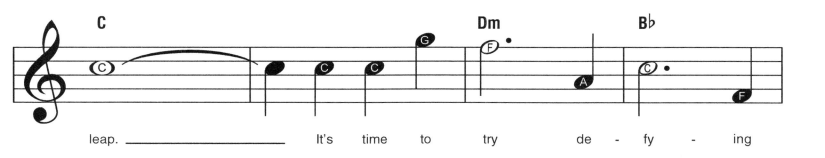

leap. _____ It's time to try de - fy - ing

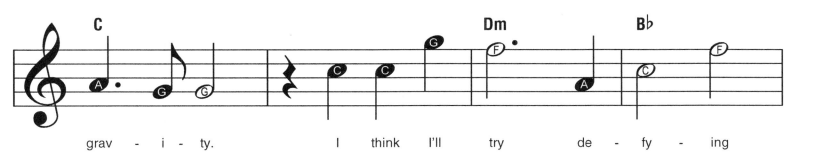

grav - i - ty. I think I'll try de - fy - ing

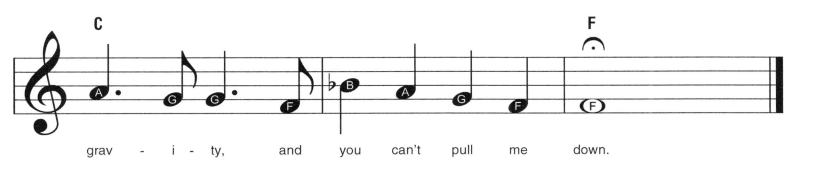

grav - i - ty, and you can't pull me down.

Do You Hear the People Sing?
from LES MISÉRABLES

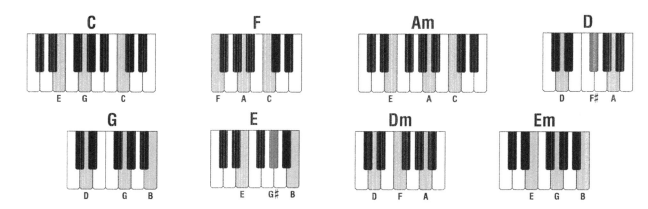

Music by Claude-Michel Schönberg
Lyrics by Alain Boublil,
Jean-Marc Natel and Herbert Kretzmer

March Shuffle

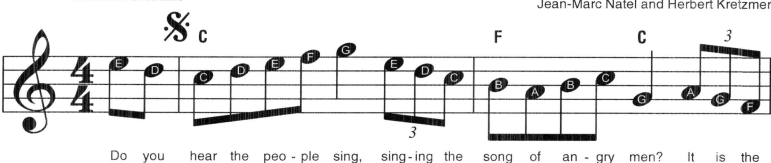

Do you hear the peo-ple sing, sing-ing the song of an-gry men? It is the

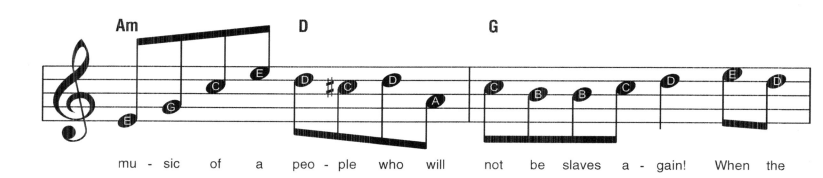

mu - sic of a peo - ple who will not be slaves a - gain! When the

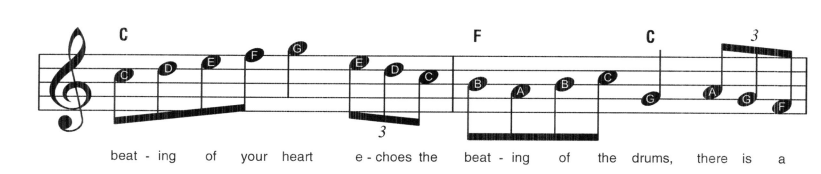

beat-ing of your heart e - choes the beat-ing of the drums, there is a

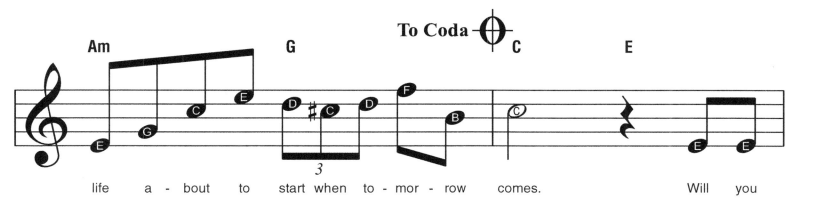

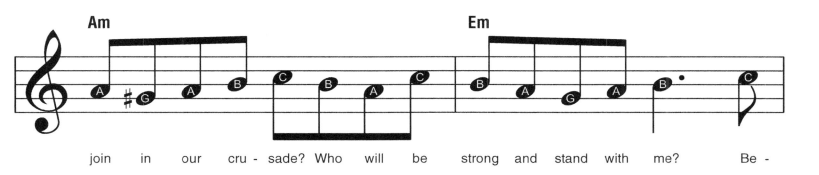

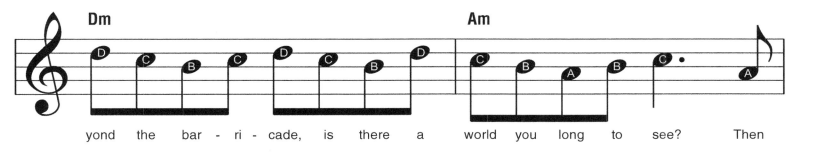

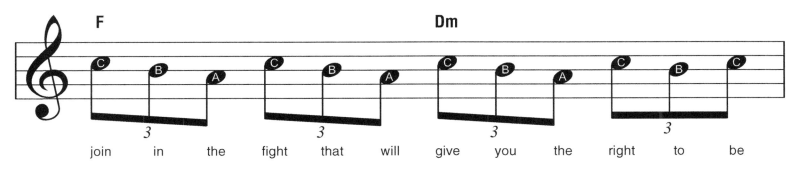

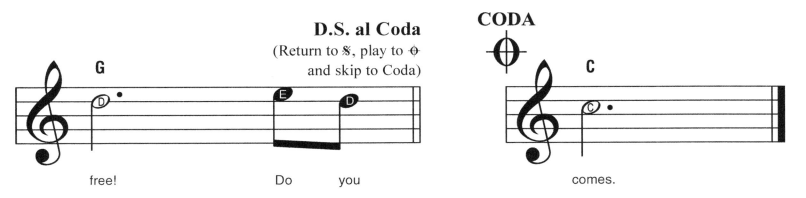

Easter Parade

featured in the Motion Picture Irving Berlin's EASTER PARADE
from AS THOUSANDS CHEER

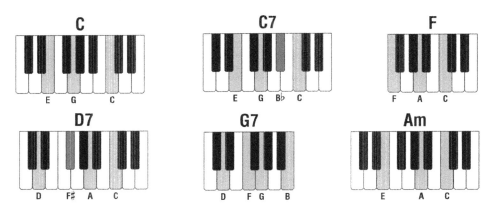

Words and Music by
Irving Berlin

Happily

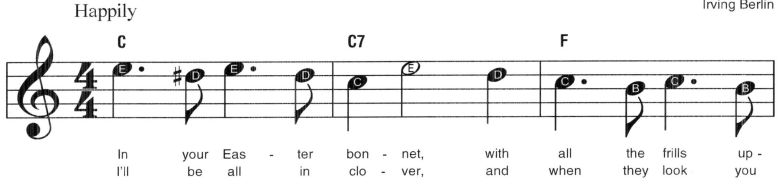

In your Eas - ter bon - net, with all the frills up -
I'll be all in clo - ver, and when they look you

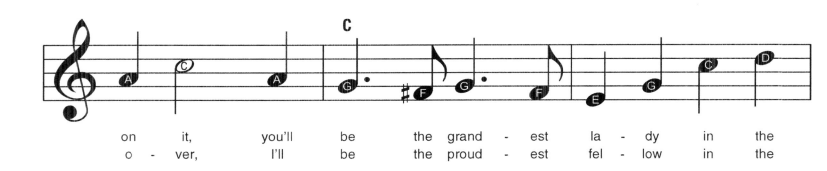

on it, you'll be the grand - est la - dy in the
o - ver, I'll be the proud - est fel - low in the

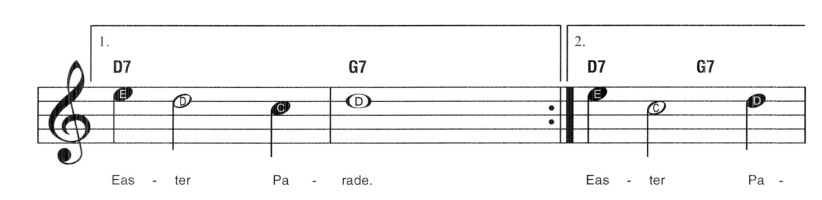

1.
Eas - ter Pa - rade.

2.
Eas - ter Pa -

33

Edelweiss
from THE SOUND OF MUSIC

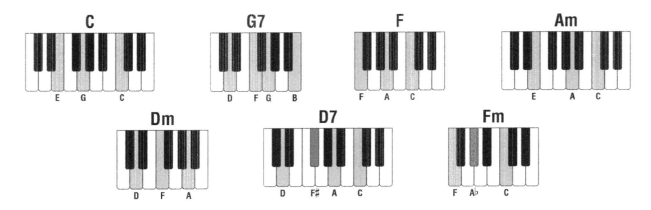

Lyrics by Oscar Hammerstein II
Music by Richard Rodgers

Simple Waltz

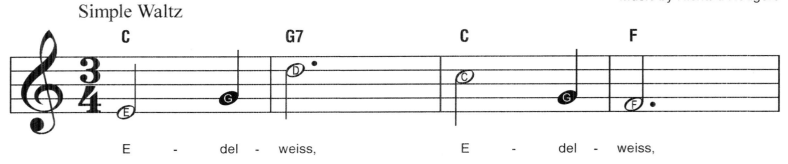

E - del - weiss, E - del - weiss,

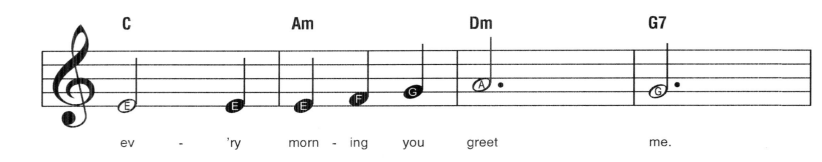

ev - 'ry morn - ing you greet me.

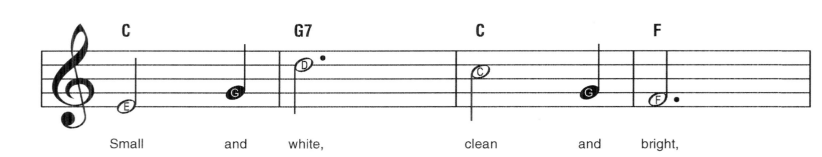

Small and white, clean and bright,

35

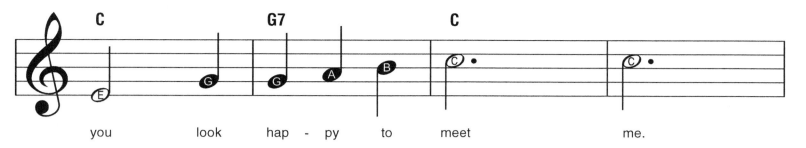

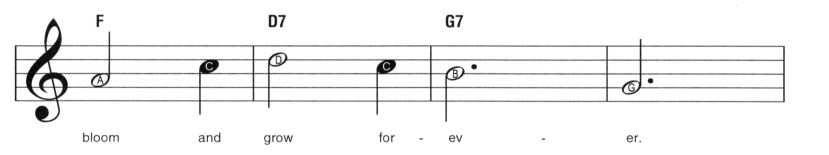

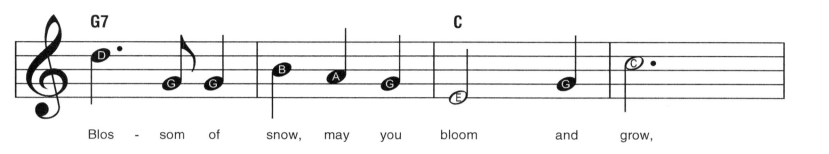

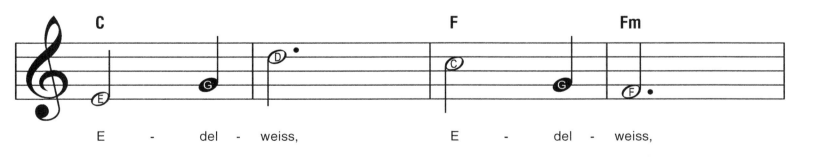

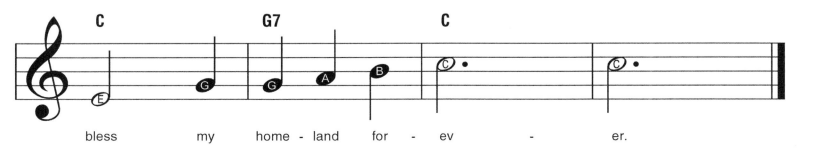

Everything's Coming Up Roses

from GYPSY

Lyrics by Stephen Sondheim
Music by Jule Styne

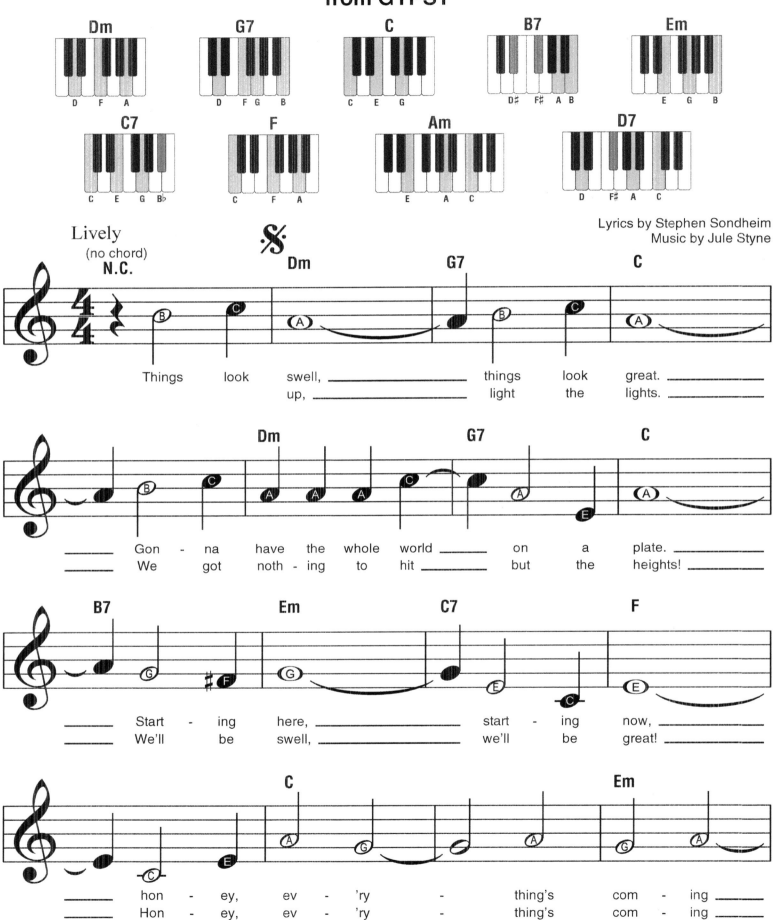

To Coda
G7
C7
up ros - es!
up ros - es
Dm
G7
C
Dm
Now's our in - ning. Stand the
G7
C
Am
world on its ear! Set it
B7
Em
Am
spin - ning. That - 'll be
D.S. al Coda
(Return to 𝄋, play to 𝄌 and skip to Coda)
D7
G7
just the be - gin - ing! Cur - tain
CODA
C
for me and for you.

Falling Slowly
from the Broadway Musical ONCE

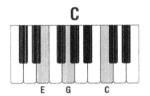
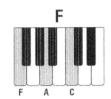
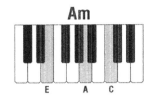

Words and Music by Glen Hansard
and Marketa Irglova

Slowly

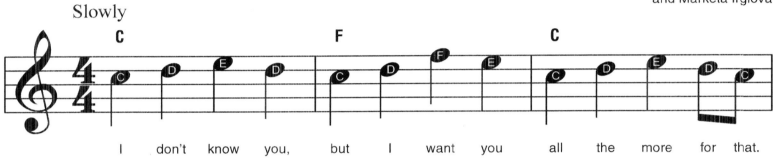

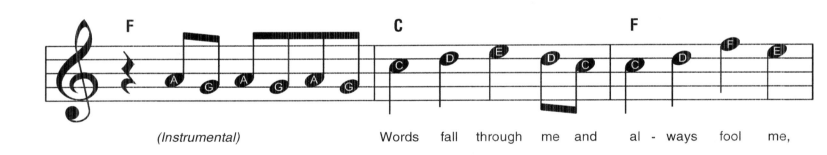

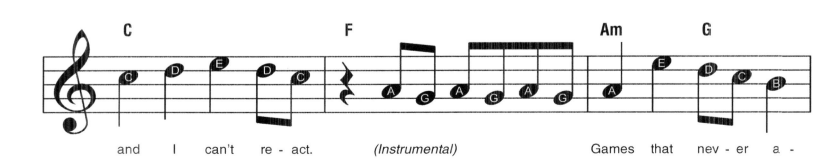

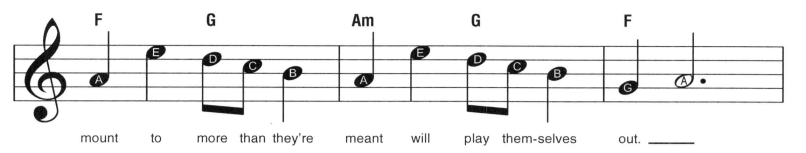

mount to more than they're meant will play them-selves out. _____

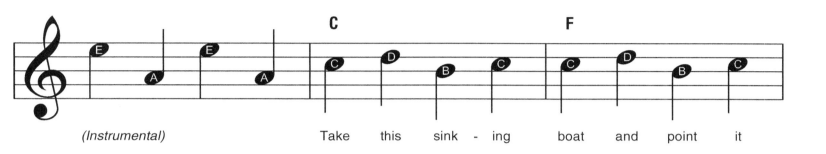

(Instrumental) Take this sink - ing boat and point it

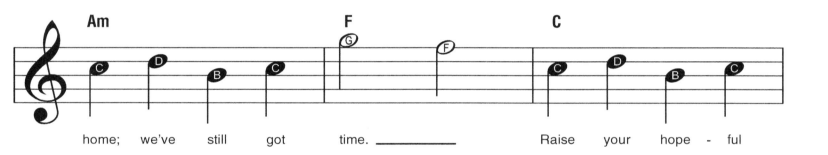

home; we've still got time. _____ Raise your hope - ful

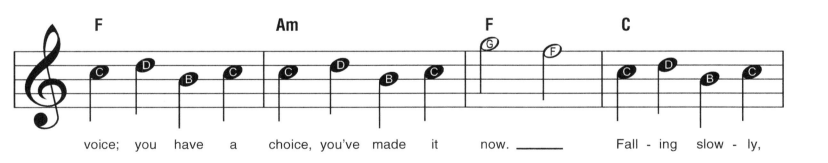

voice; you have a choice, you've made it now. _____ Fall - ing slow - ly,

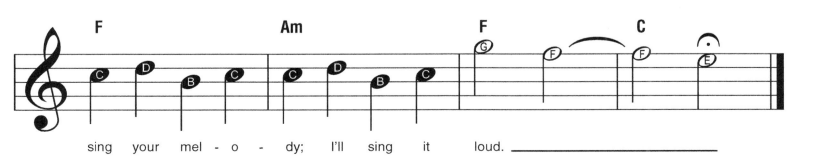

sing your mel - o - dy; I'll sing it loud. _____

Footloose

from the Broadway Musical FOOTLOOSE

Words by Dean Pitchford
Music by Kenny Loggins

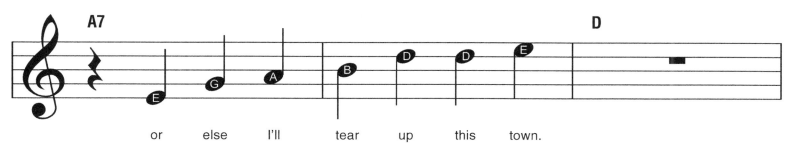

or else I'll tear up this town.

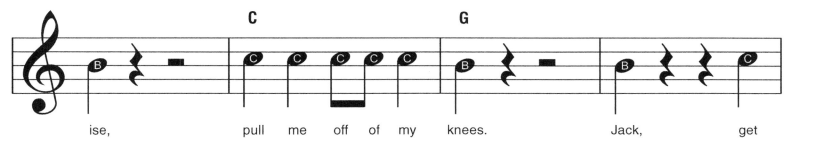

To - night I got - ta cut loose, foot - loose;

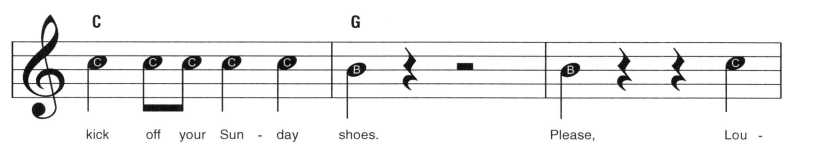

kick off your Sun - day shoes. Please, Lou -

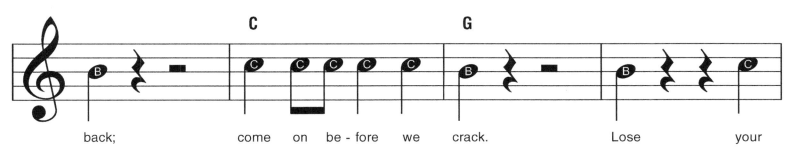

ise, pull me off of my knees. Jack, get

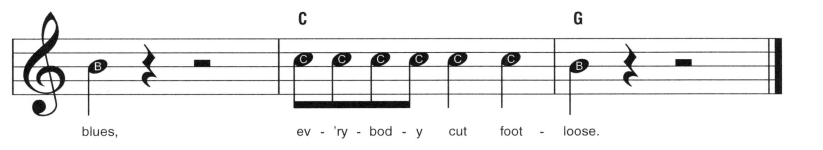

back; come on be - fore we crack. Lose your

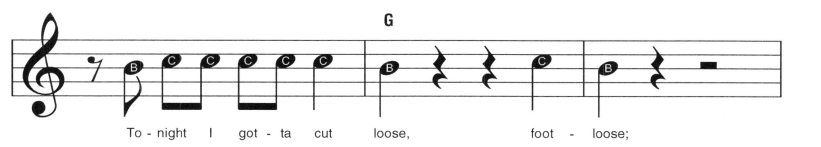

blues, ev - 'ry - bod - y cut foot - loose.

Gonna Build a Mountain

from the Musical Production STOP THE WORLD – I WANT TO GET OFF

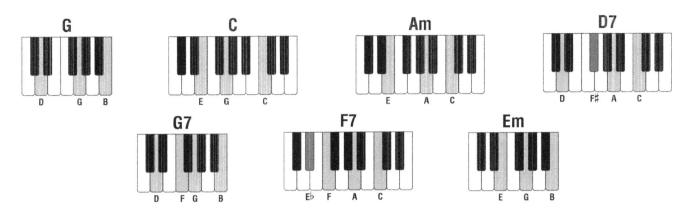

Words and Music by Leslie Bricusse
and Anthony Newley

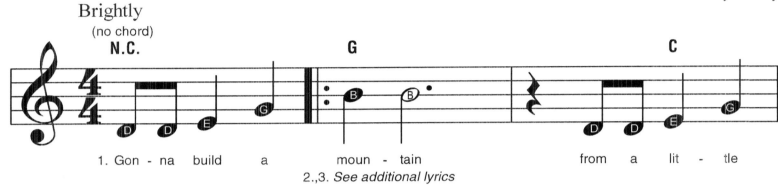

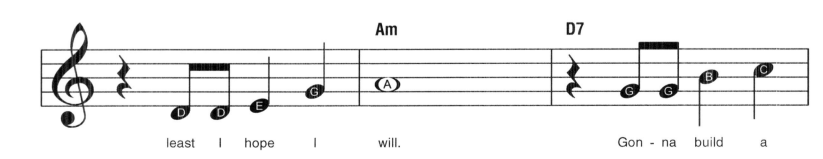

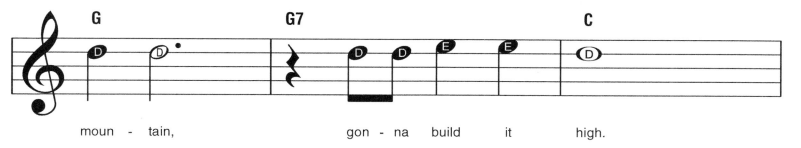

moun - tain,   gon - na   build   it   high.

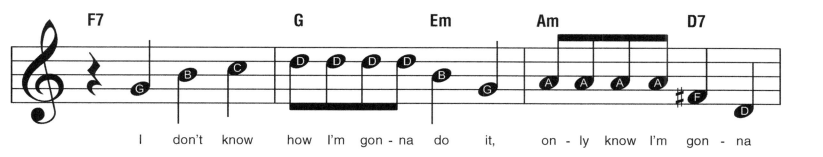

I   don't   know   how I'm gon - na   do   it,   on - ly know I'm   gon - na

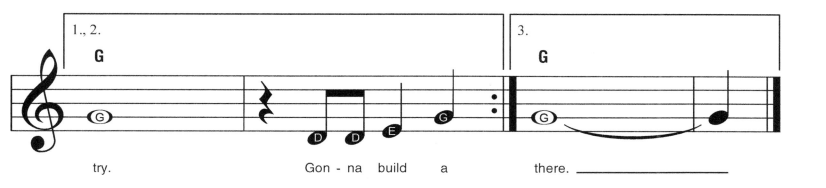

1., 2.   3.

try.   Gon - na build   a   there. _____

Additional Lyrics

2. Gonna build a daydream from a little hope.
   Gonna push that daydream up the mountain slope.
   Gonna build a daydream, gonna see it through.
   Gonna build a mountain and a daydream, gonna make 'em both come true.

3. Gonna build a heaven from a little hell.
   Gonna build a heaven, and I know darn well,
   If I build my mountain with a lot of care,
   And take my daydream up the mountain, heaven will be waiting there.

Good Morning Starshine
from the Broadway Musical Production HAIR

Words by James Rado
and Gerome Ragni
Music by Galt MacDermot

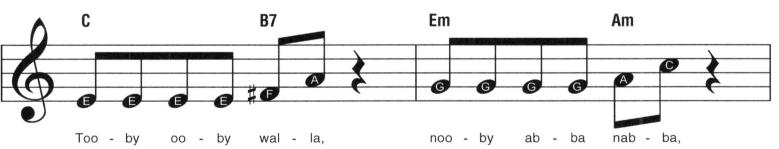
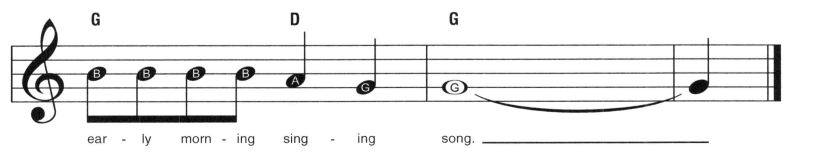

Goodnight, My Someone
from Meredith Willson's THE MUSIC MAN

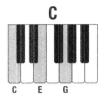 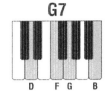 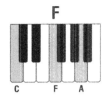 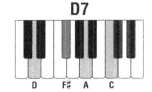

By Meredith Willson

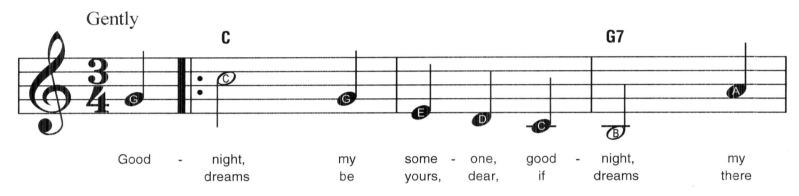

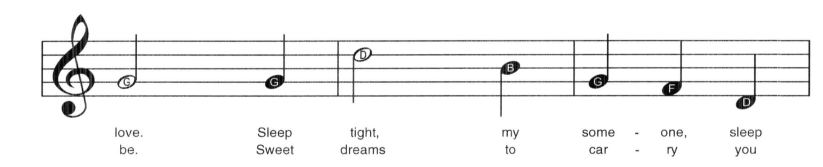

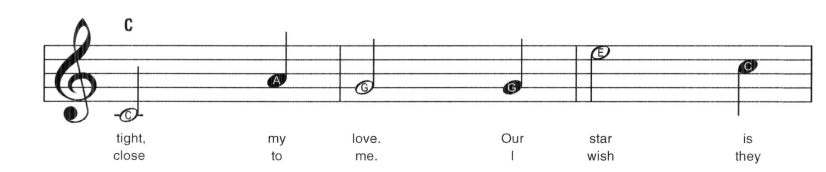

Happy Talk
from SOUTH PACIFIC

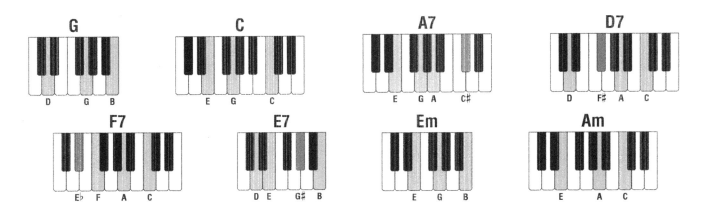

Lyrics by Oscar Hammerstein II
Music by Richard Rodgers

Brightly

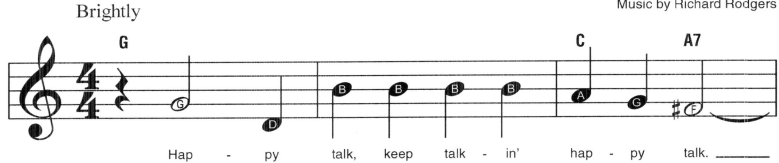

Hap - py talk, keep talk - in' hap - py talk. _____

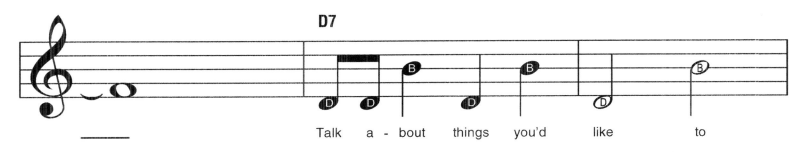

_____ Talk a - bout things you'd like to

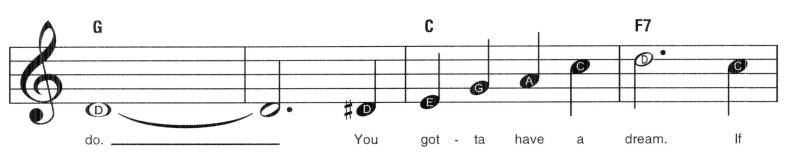

do. _____ You got - ta have a dream. If

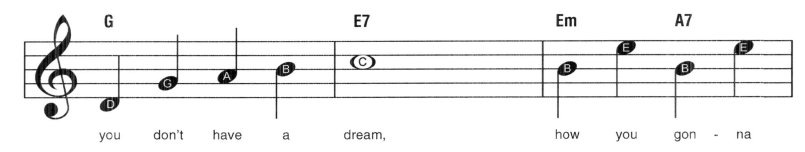

you don't have a dream, how you gon - na

49

Heart

from DAMN YANKEES

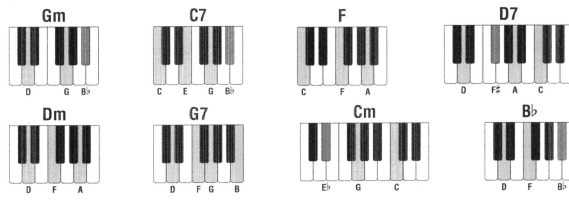

Words and Music by Richard Adler
and Jerry Ross

Moderate Shuffle

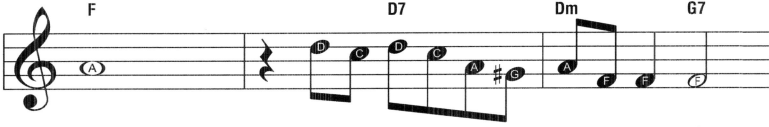

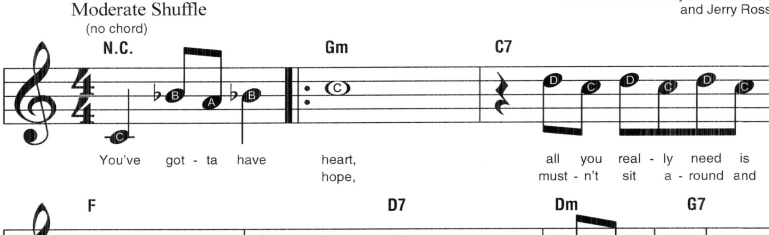

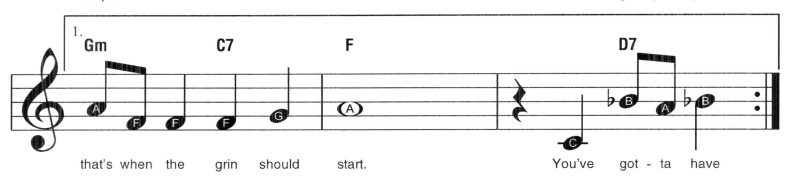

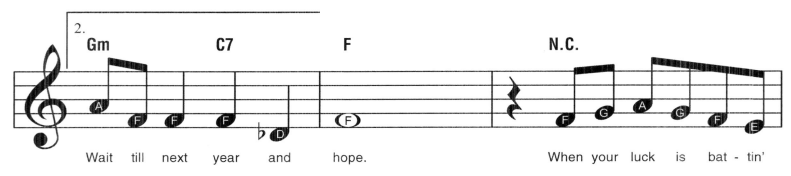

Hello, Dolly!
from HELLO, DOLLY!

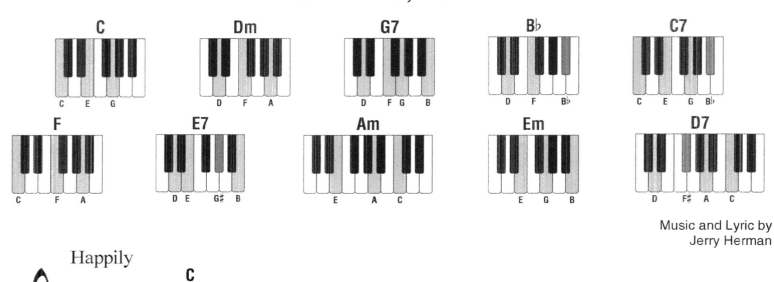

Music and Lyric by
Jerry Herman

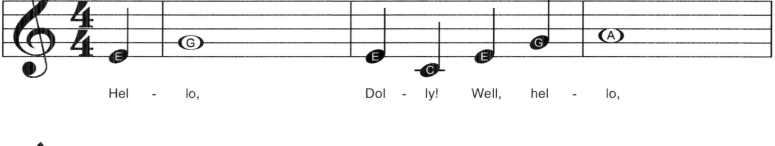

Hel - lo, Dol - ly! Well, hel - lo,

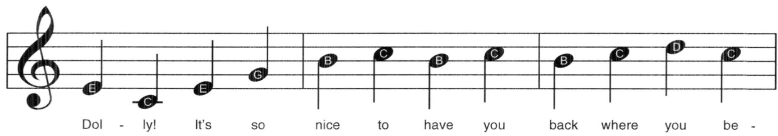

Dol - ly! It's so nice to have you back where you be -

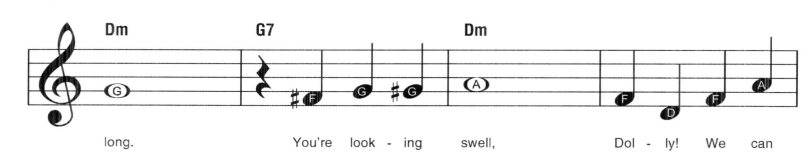

long. You're look - ing swell, Dol - ly! We can

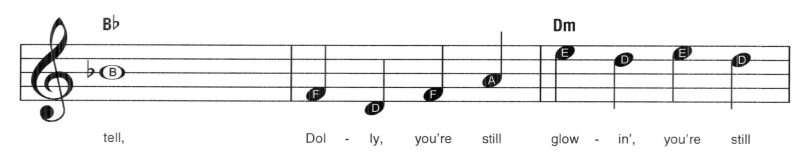

tell, Dol - ly, you're still glow - in', you're still

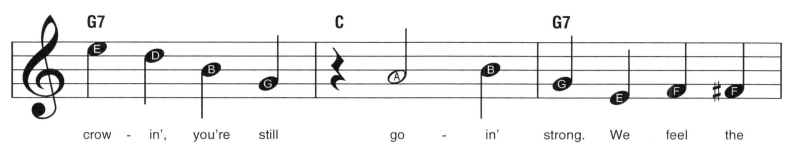

crow - in', you're still go - in' strong. We feel the

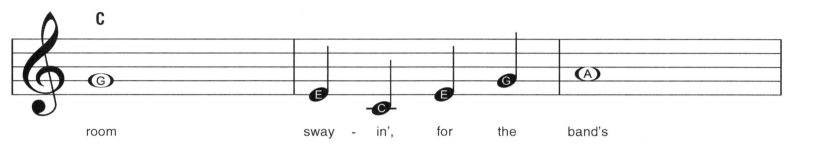

room sway - in', for the band's

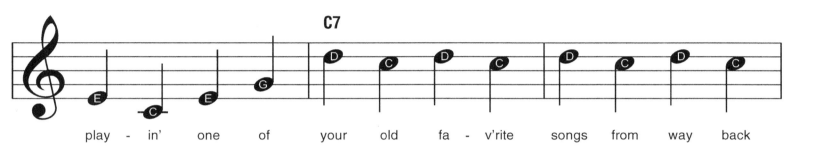

play - in' one of your old fa - v'rite songs from way back

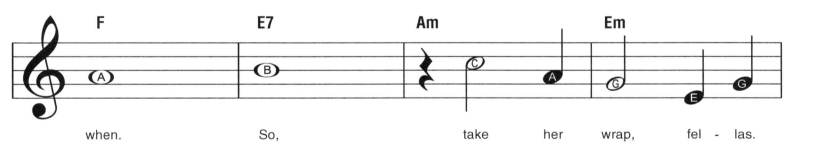

when. So, take her wrap, fel - las.

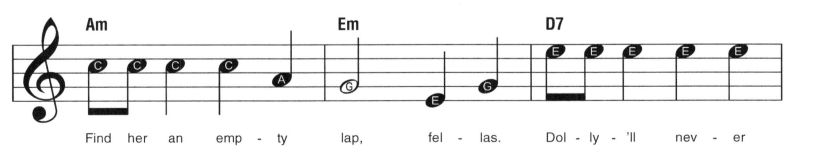

Find her an emp - ty lap, fel - las. Dol - ly - 'll nev - er

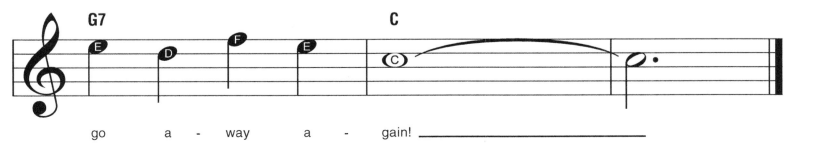

go a - way a - gain! _____

Hello, Young Lovers
from THE KING AND I

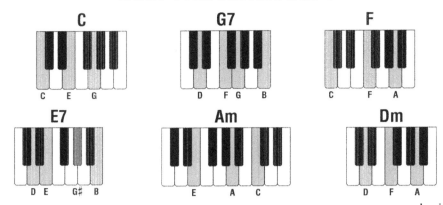

Lyrics by Oscar Hammerstein II
Music by Richard Rodgers

Happy Waltz

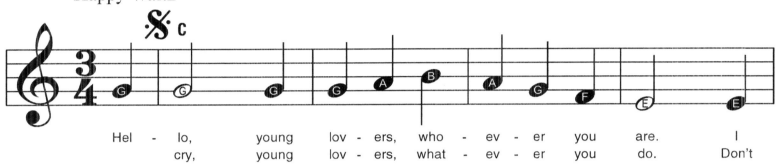

Hel - lo, young lov - ers, who - ev - er you are. I
cry, young lov - ers, what - ev - er you do. Don't

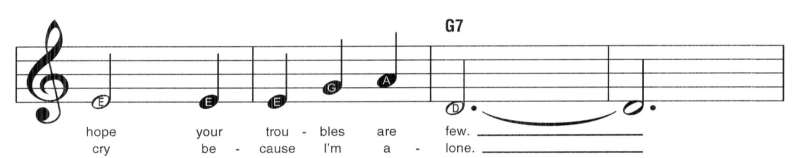

hope your trou - bles are few. _____
cry be - cause I'm a - lone. _____

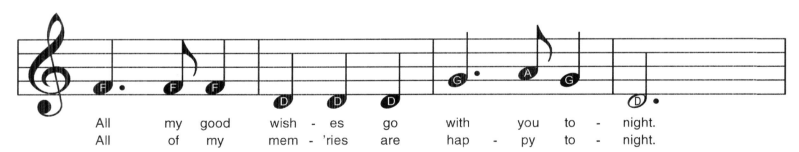

All my good wish - es go with you to - night.
All of my mem - 'ries are hap - py to - night.

To Coda

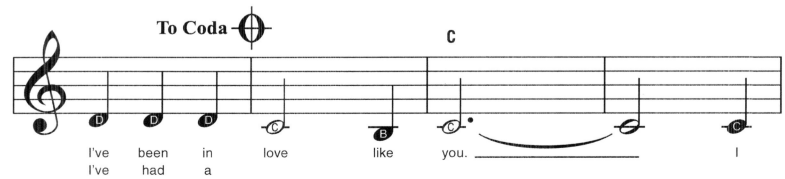

I've been in love like you. _____ I
I've had a

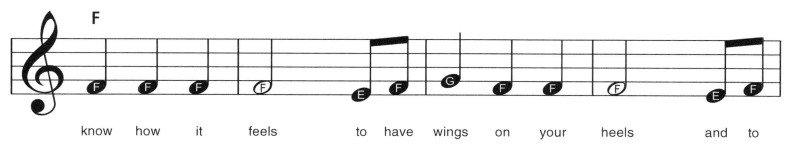

know how it feels to have wings on your heels and to

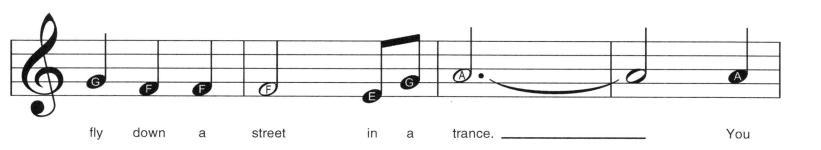

fly down a street in a trance. _____ You

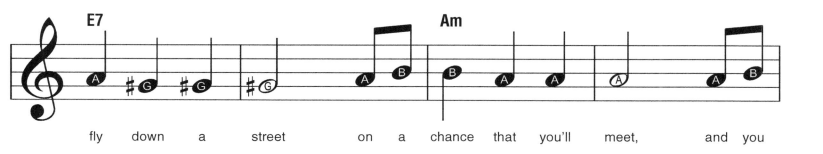

fly down a street on a chance that you'll meet, and you

D.S. al Coda
(Return to 𝄋, play to ⊕
and skip to Coda)

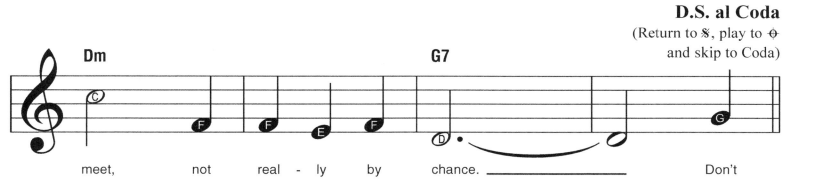

meet, not real - ly by chance. _____ Don't

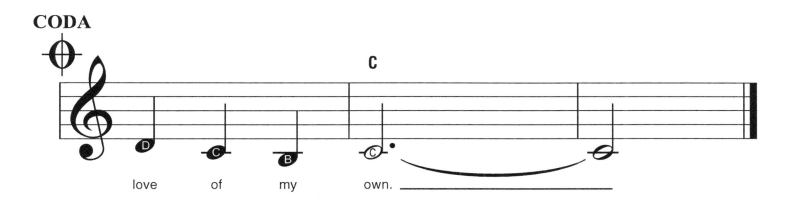

love of my own. _____

How Are Things in Glocca Morra
from FINIAN'S RAINBOW

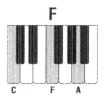
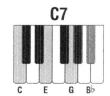
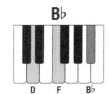
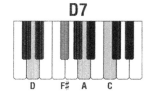
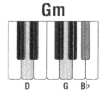

Words by E.Y. "Yip" Harburg
Music by Burton Lane

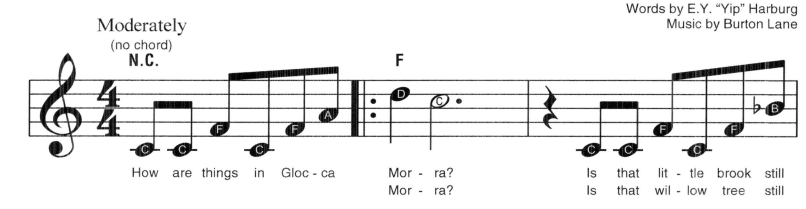

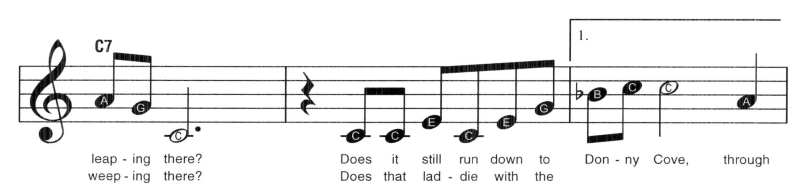

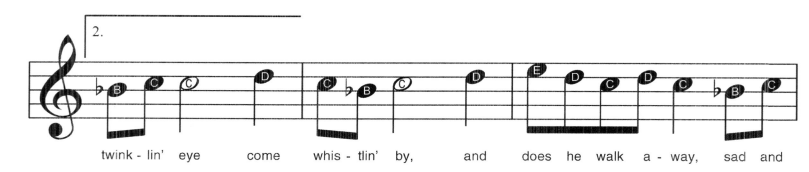

57

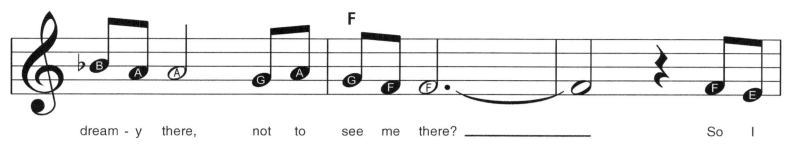

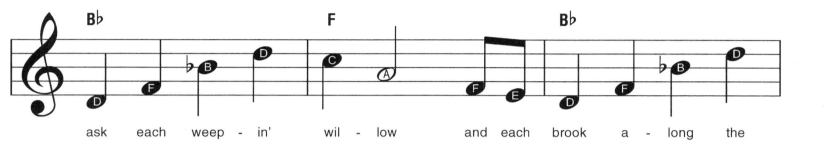

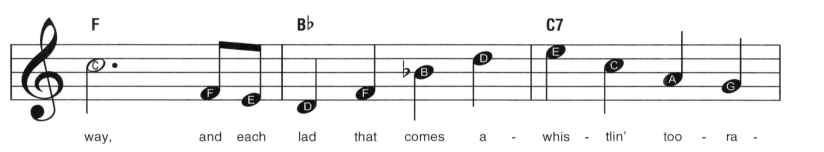

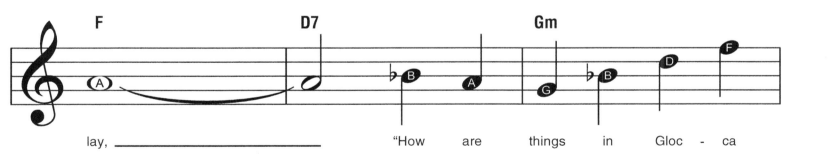

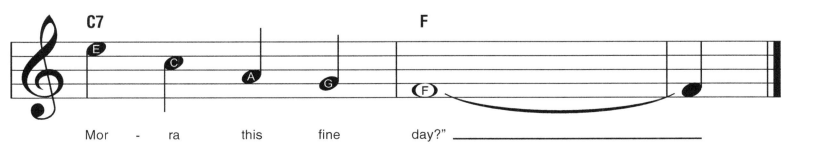

I Could Have Danced All Night

from MY FAIR LADY

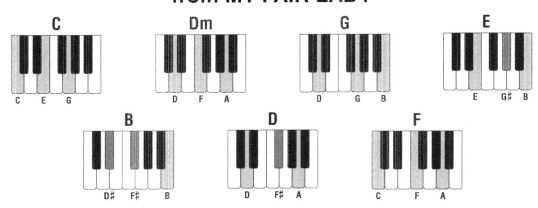

Words by Alan Jay Lerner
Music by Frederick Loewe

Happily

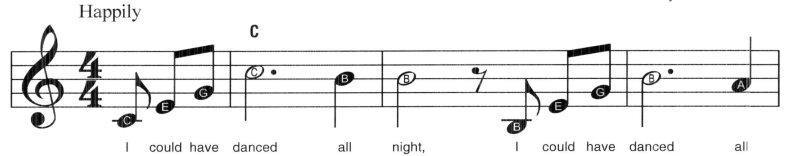

I could have danced all night, I could have danced all

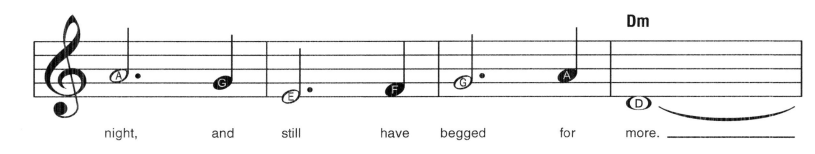

night, and still have begged for more. _____

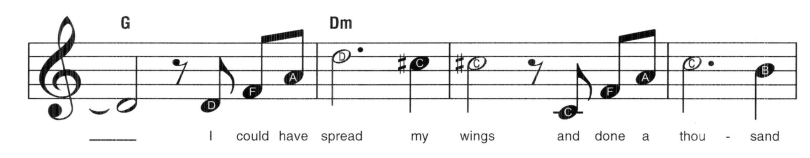

_____ I could have spread my wings and done a thou - sand

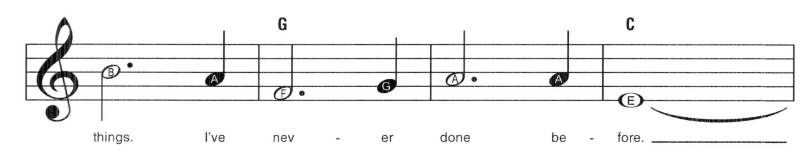

things. I've nev - er done be - fore. _____

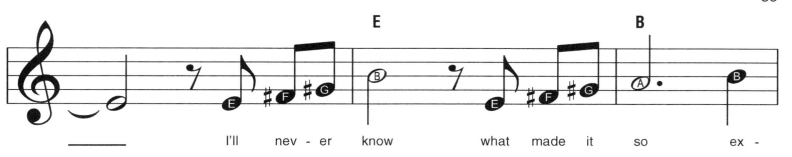

I'll nev - er know what made it so ex -

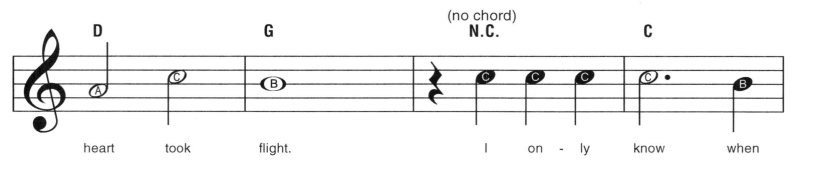

cit - ing, _____ why all at once my

heart took flight. I on - ly know when

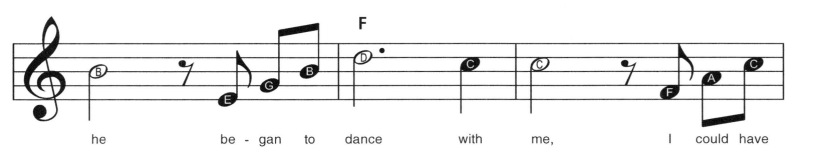

he be - gan to dance with me, I could have

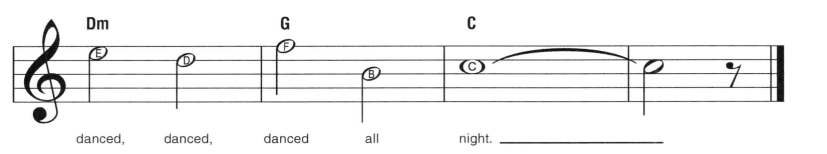

danced, danced, danced all night. _____

I Enjoy Being a Girl

from FLOWER DRUM SONG

Lyrics by Oscar Hammerstein II
Music by Richard Rodgers

61

I Only Have Eyes for You

from DAMES

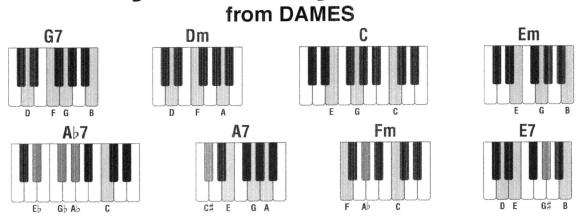

Words by Al Dubin
Music by Harry Warren

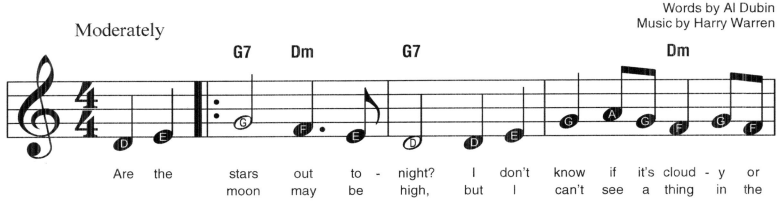

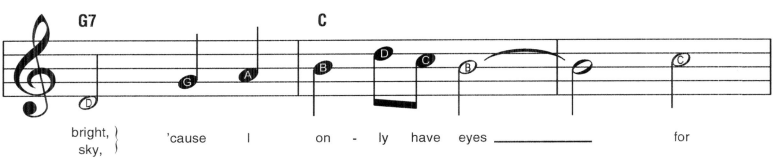

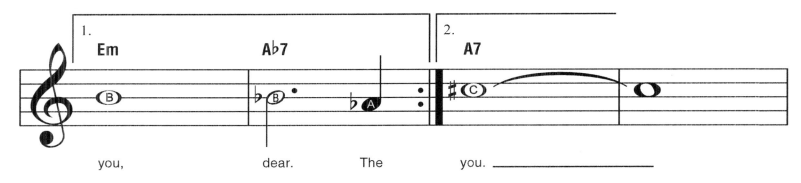

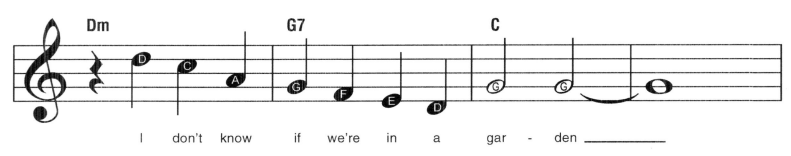

63

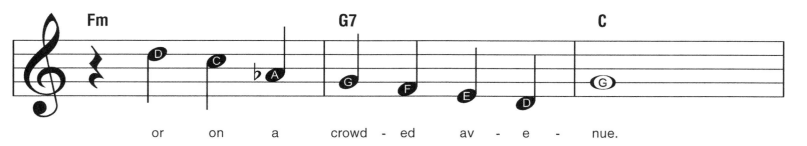

or on a crowd - ed av - e - nue.

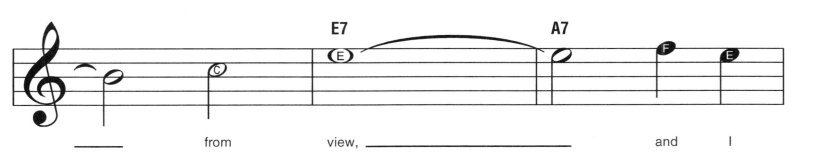

You are here, so am I. May - be

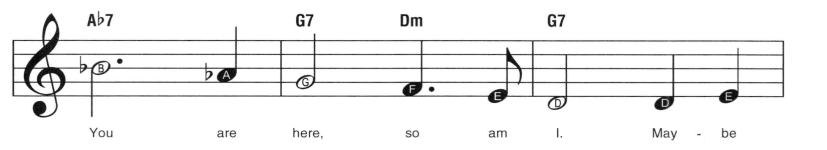

mil - lions of peo - ple go by, but they all dis - ap - pear _____

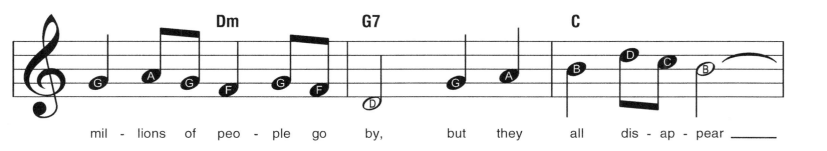

_____ from view, _____ and I

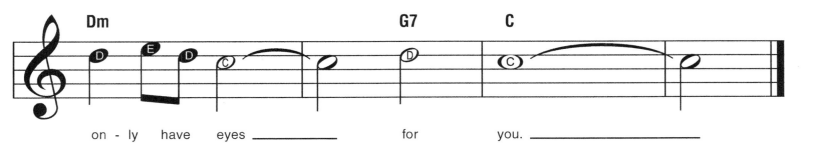

on - ly have eyes _____ for you. _____

If I Were a Bell
from GUYS AND DOLLS

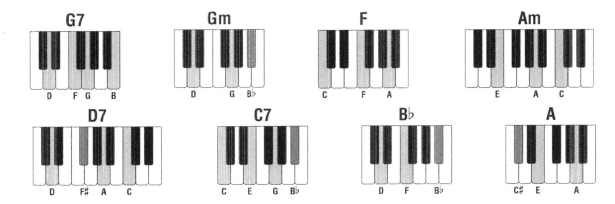

By Frank Loesser

Ask me how do I feel, ask me now that we're co- zy and
how do I feel, lit- tle me with my qui- et up-

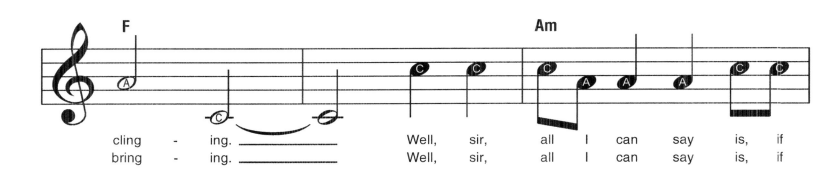

cling - ing. _____ Well, sir, all I can say is, if
bring - ing. _____ Well, sir, all I can say is, if

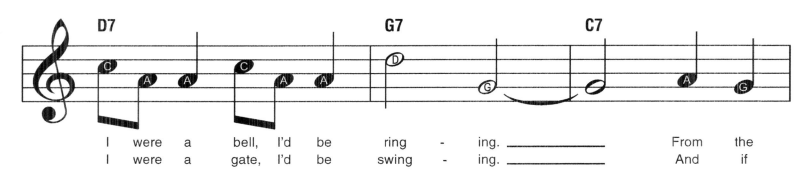

I were a bell, I'd be ring - ing. _____ From the
I were a gate, I'd be swing - ing. _____ And if

65

It Might as Well Be Spring

from STATE FAIR

Lyrics by Oscar Hammerstein II
Music by Richard Rodgers

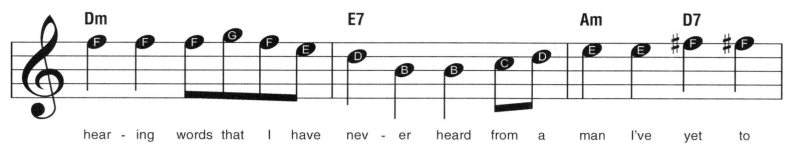

hear - ing words that I have nev - er heard from a man I've yet to

D.S. al Coda
(Return to %, play to ⊕
and skip to Coda)

CODA

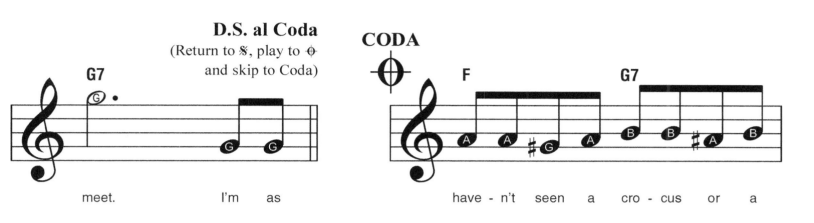

meet. I'm as

have - n't seen a cro - cus or a

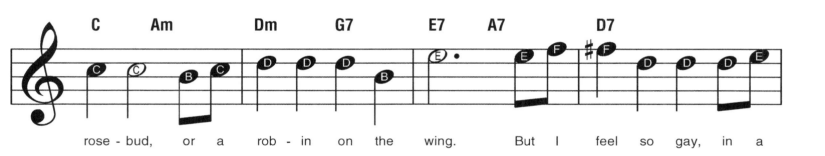

rose - bud, or a rob - in on the wing. But I feel so gay, in a

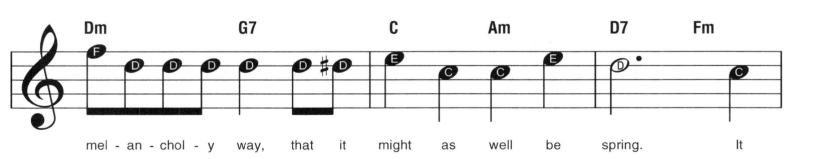

mel - an - chol - y way, that it might as well be spring. It

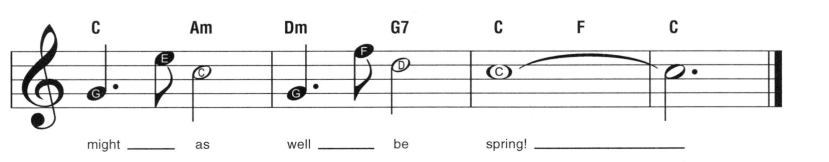

might _____ as well _____ be spring! _____

Lullaby of Broadway
from 42ND STREET

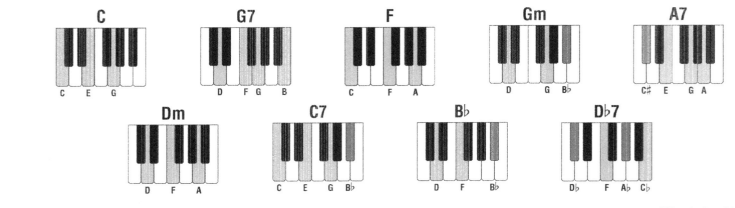

Words by Al Dubin
Music by Harry Warren

Easy Shuffle feel

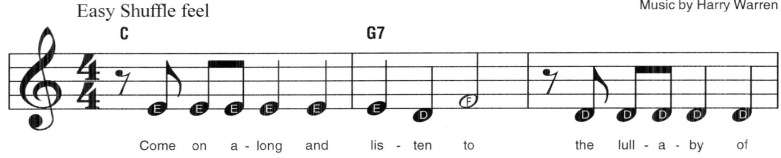

Come on a-long and lis-ten to the lull-a-by of

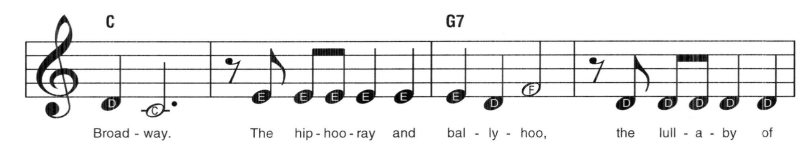

Broad-way. The hip-hoo-ray and bal-ly-hoo, the lull-a-by of

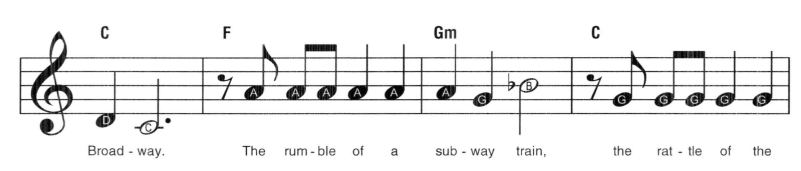

Broad-way. The rum-ble of a sub-way train, the rat-tle of the

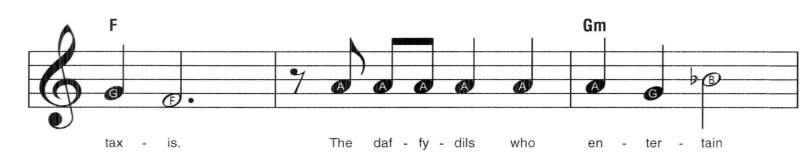

tax-is. The daf-fy-dils who en-ter-tain

Memory

from CATS

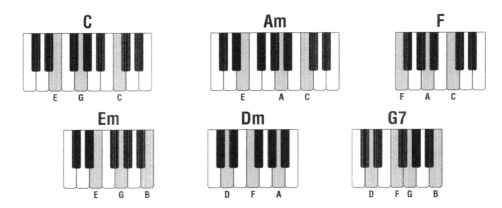

Music by Andrew Lloyd Webber
Text by Trevor Nunn after T.S. Eliot

Flowing

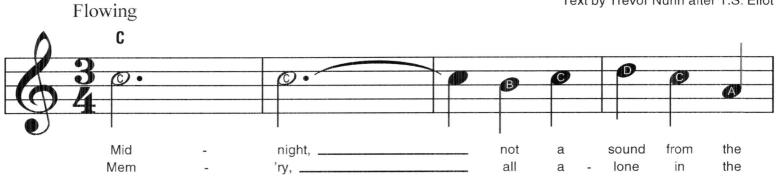

Mid - night, _____ not a sound from the
Mem - 'ry, _____ all a - lone in the

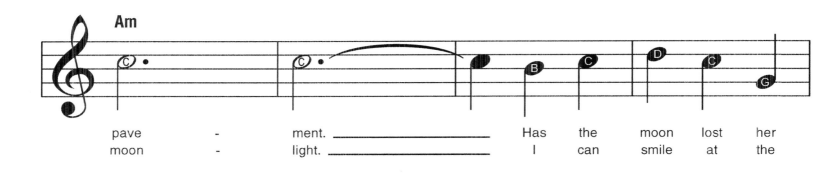

pave - ment. _____ Has the moon lost her
moon - light. _____ I can smile at the

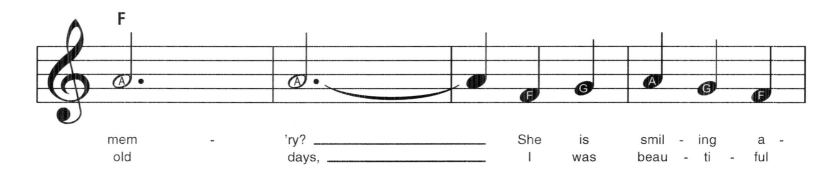

mem - 'ry? _____ She is smil - ing a -
old days, _____ I was beau - ti - ful

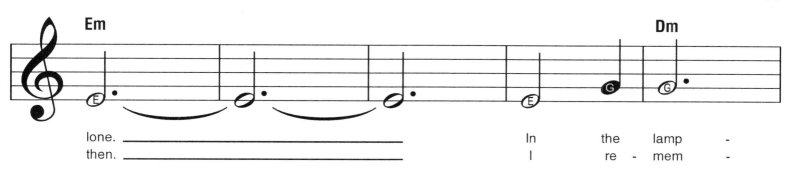

lone. _____ In the lamp -
then. _____ I re - mem -

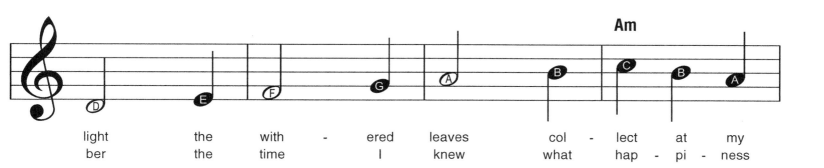

light   the   with - ered   leaves   col - lect   at   my
ber   the   with   time   I   knew   what   hap - pi - ness

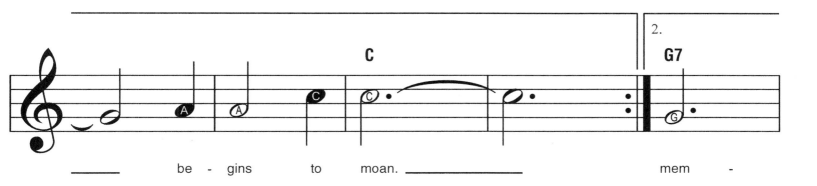

feet, _____   and   the   wind _____
was. _____   Let   the

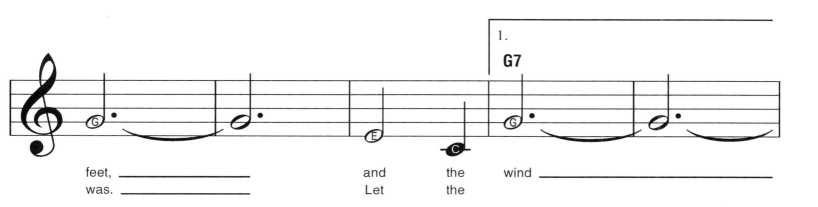

_____   be - gins   to   moan. _____   mem -

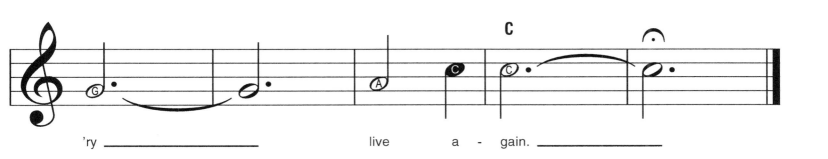

'ry _____   live   a - gain. _____

The Music of the Night
from THE PHANTOM OF THE OPERA

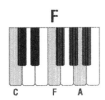 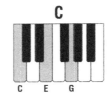 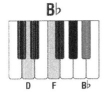

Music by Andrew Lloyd Webber
Lyrics by Charles Hart
Additional Lyrics by Richard Stilgoe

Slowly, with much expression

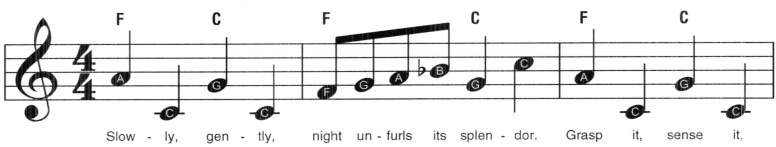

Slow - ly, gen - tly, night un - furls its splen - dor. Grasp it, sense it,

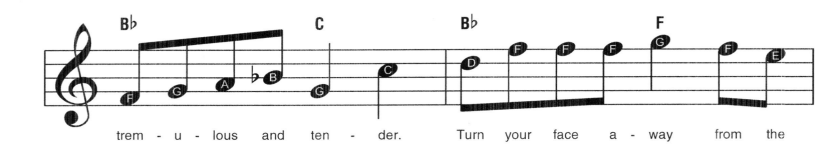

trem - u - lous and ten - der. Turn your face a - way from the

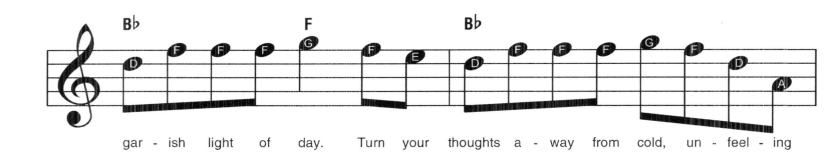

gar - ish light of day. Turn your thoughts a - way from cold, un - feel - ing

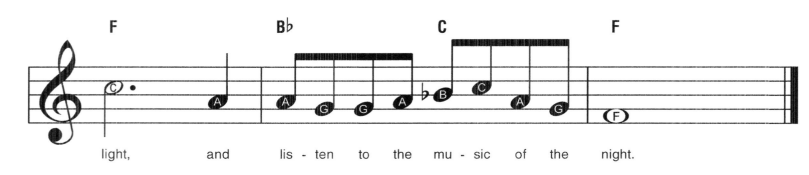

light, and lis - ten to the mu - sic of the night.

New York, New York
from ON THE TOWN

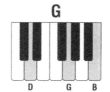
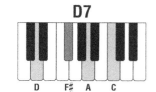
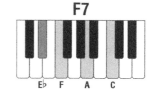
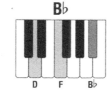

Lyrics by Betty Comden
and Adolph Green
Music by Leonard Bernstein

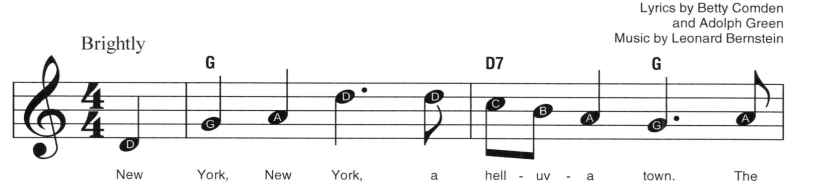

New York, New York, a hell - uv - a town. The

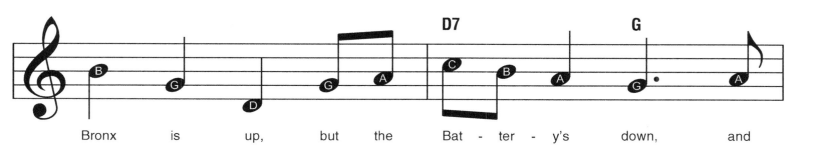

Bronx is up, but the Bat - ter - y's down, and

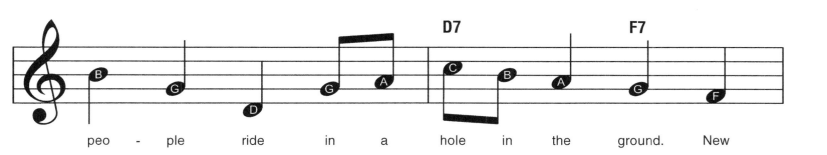

peo - ple ride in a hole in the ground. New

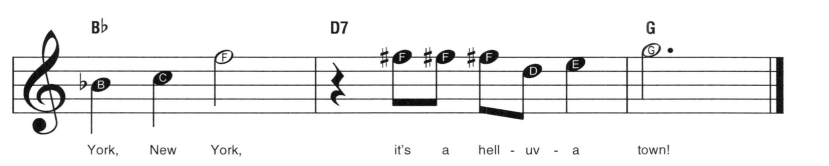

York, New York, it's a hell - uv - a town!

Never Never Land

from PETER PAN

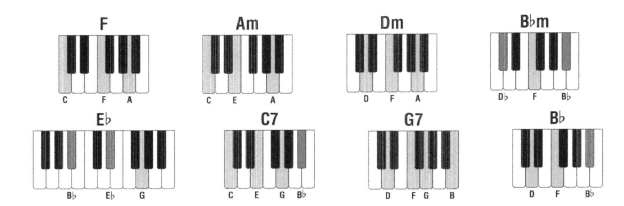

Lyric by Betty Comden
and Adolph Green
Music by Jule Styne

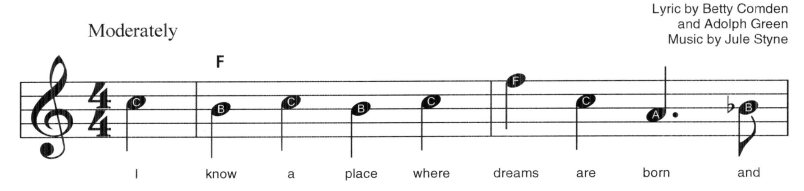

I know a place where dreams are born and

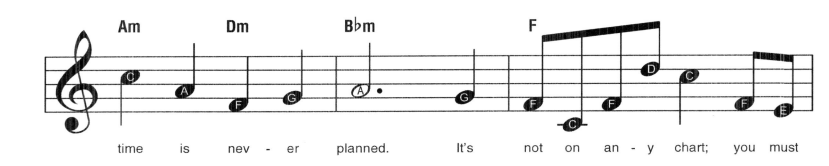

time is nev - er planned. It's not on an - y chart; you must

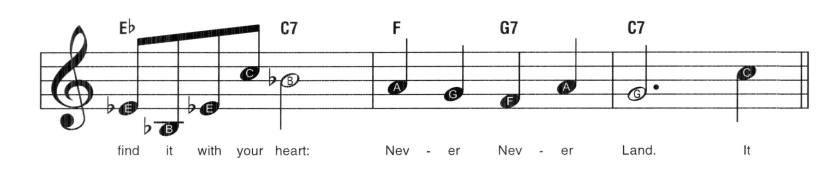

find it with your heart: Nev - er Nev - er Land. It

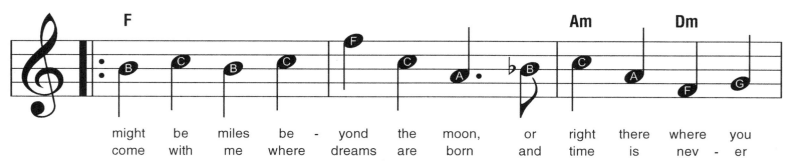

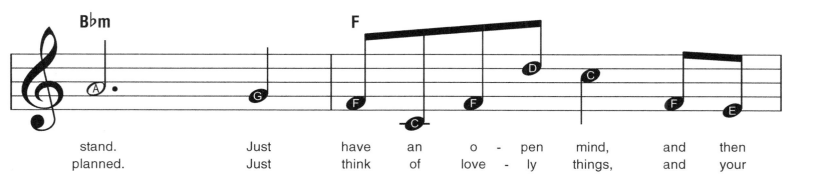

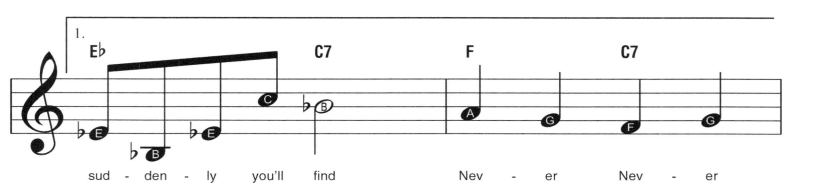

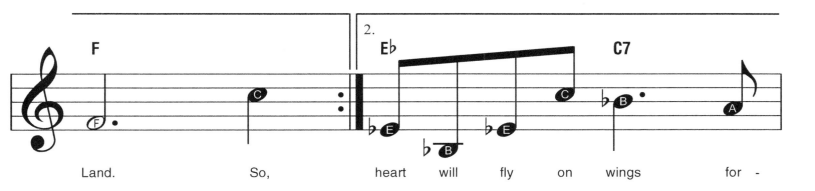

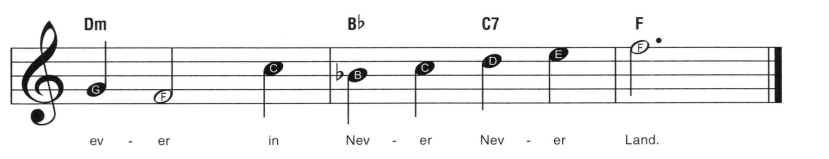

Oh, What a Beautiful Mornin'

from OKLAHOMA!

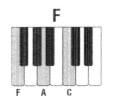

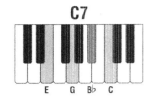

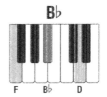

Lyrics by Oscar Hammerstein II
Music by Richard Rodgers

Happy Waltz

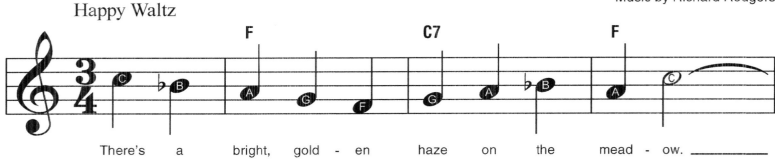

There's a bright, gold - en haze on the mead - ow. _____

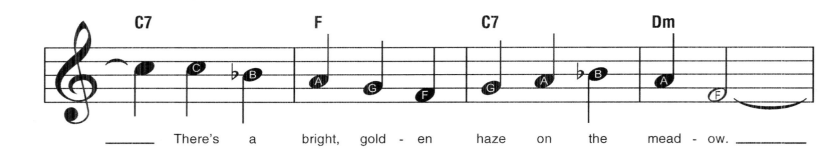

_____ There's a bright, gold - en haze on the mead - ow. _____

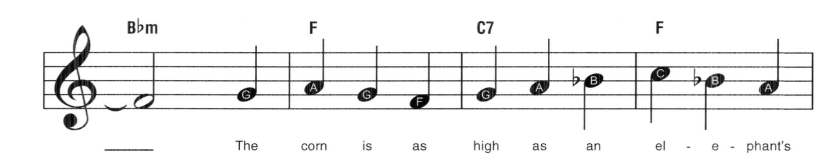

_____ The corn is as high as an el - e - phant's

77

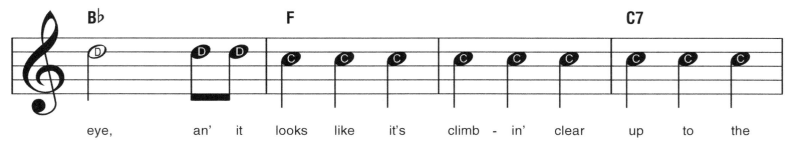

eye,   an' it   looks   like   it's   climb - in'   clear   up   to   the

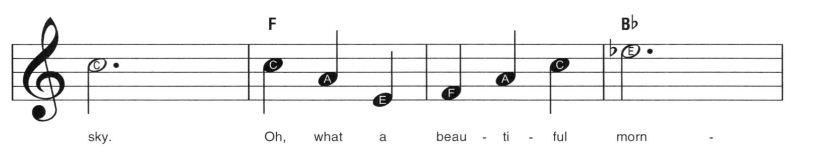

sky.   Oh,   what   a   beau - ti - ful   morn -

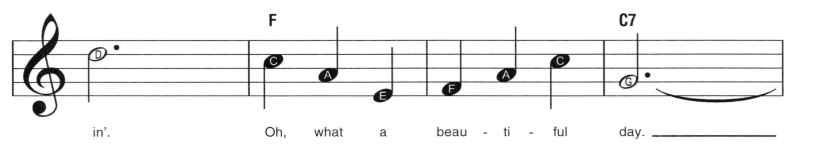

in'.   Oh,   what   a   beau - ti - ful   day. _____

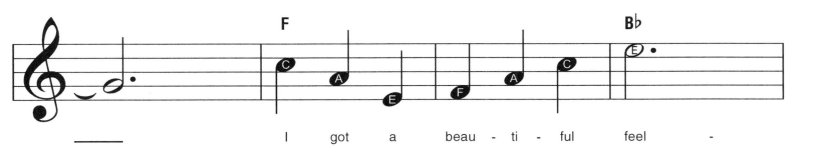

_____   I   got   a   beau - ti - ful   feel -

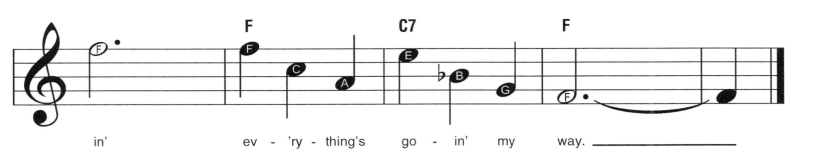

in'   ev - 'ry - thing's   go - in'   my   way. _____

Ol' Man River

from SHOW BOAT

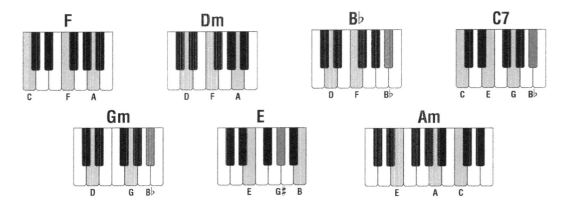

Lyrics by Oscar Hammerstein II
Music by Jerome Kern

Moderately

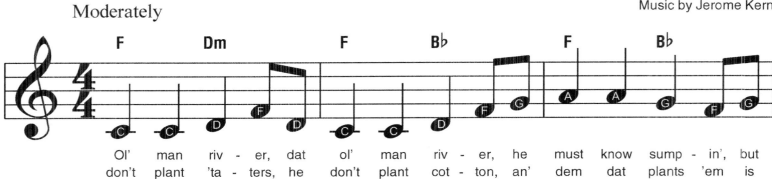

Ol' man riv - er, dat ol' man riv - er, he must know sump - in', but
don't plant 'ta - ters, he don't plant cot - ton, an' dem dat plants 'em is

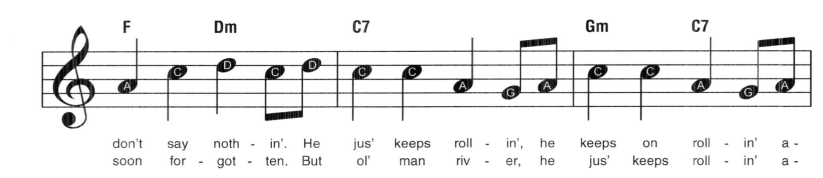

don't say noth - in'. He jus' keeps roll - in', he keeps on roll - in' a -
soon for - got - ten. But ol' man riv - er, he jus' keeps roll - in' a -

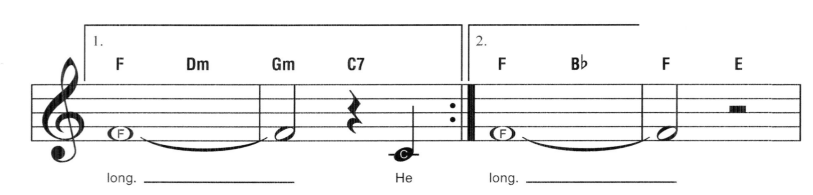

1.
long. _____

He

2.
long. _____

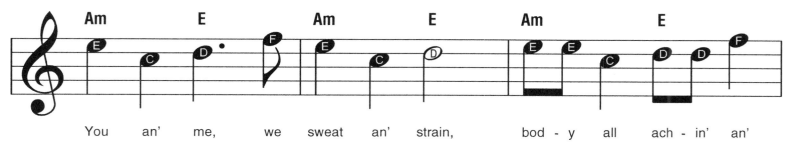

You an' me, we sweat an' strain, bod-y all ach-in' an'

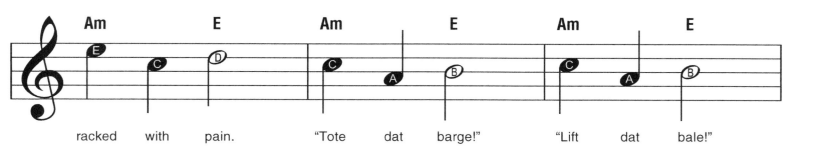

racked with pain. "Tote dat barge!" "Lift dat bale!"

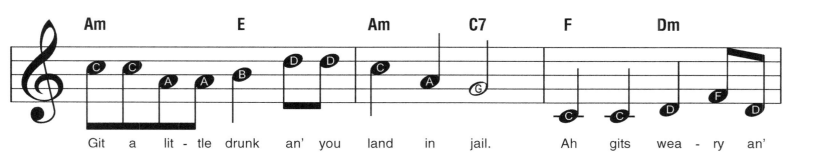

Git a lit-tle drunk an' you land in jail. Ah gits wea-ry an'

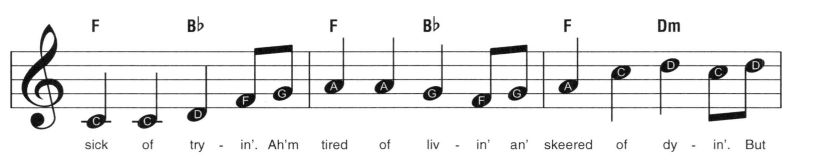

sick of try-in'. Ah'm tired of liv-in' an' skeered of dy-in'. But

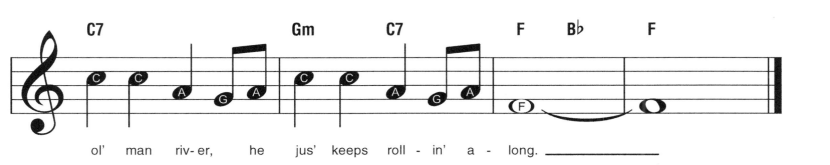

ol' man riv-er, he jus' keeps roll-in' a-long. _____

On a Clear Day
(You Can See Forever)
from ON A CLEAR DAY YOU CAN SEE FOREVER

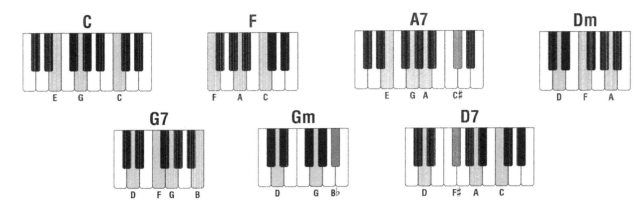

Words by Alan Jay Lerner
Music by Burton Lane

Moderately

On a clear day, _____ rise and look a - round you, _____

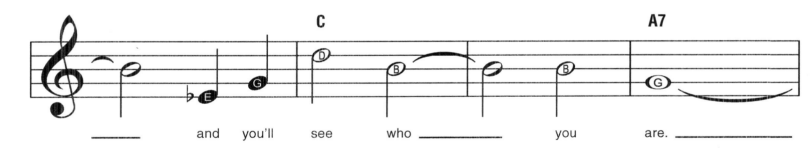

_____ and you'll see who _____ you are. _____

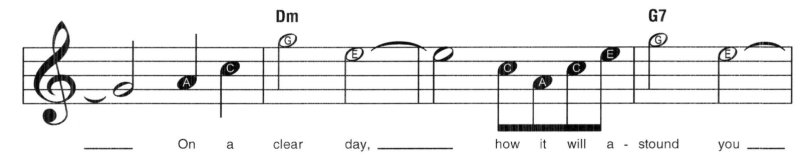

_____ On a clear day, _____ how it will a - stound you _____

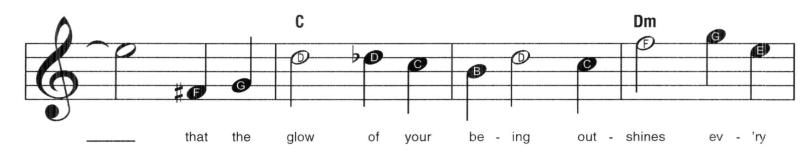

_____ that the glow of your be - ing out - shines ev - 'ry

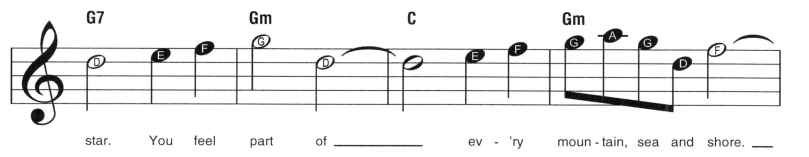

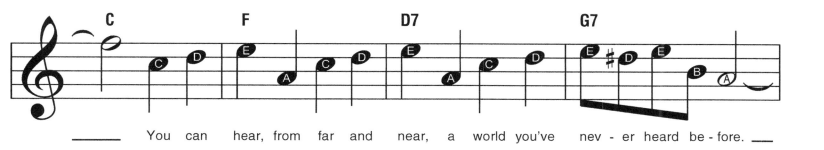

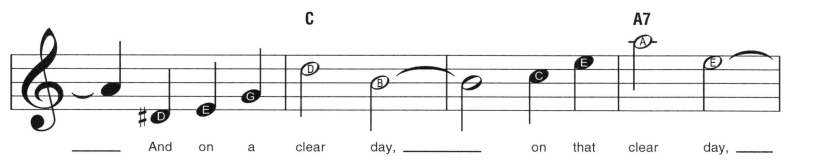

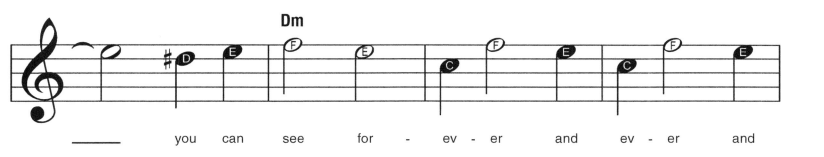

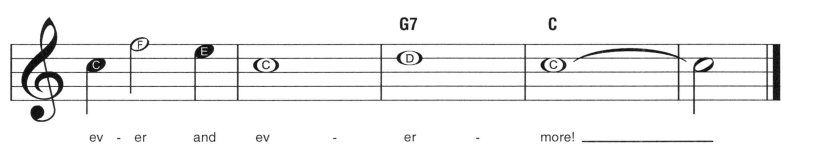

On My Own
from LES MISÉRABLES

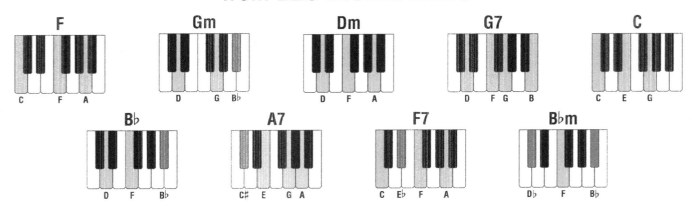

Music by Claude-Michel Schönberg
Lyrics by Alain Boublil,
Jean-Marc Natel, Herbert Kretzmer,
John Caird and Trevor Nunn

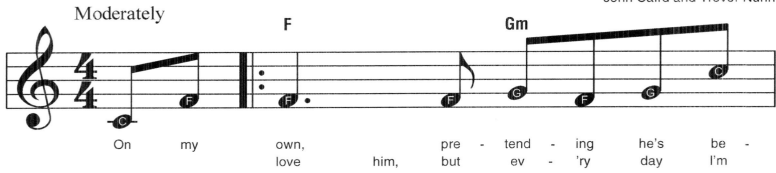

On my own, pre - tend - ing he's be -
love him, but ev - 'ry day I'm

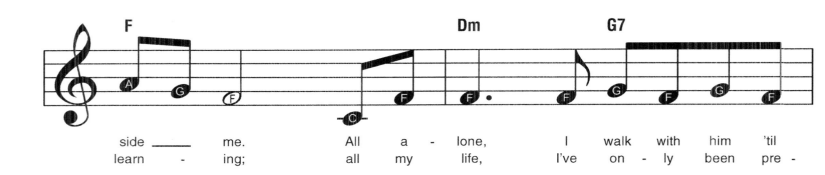

side _____ me. All a - lone, I walk with him 'til
learn - ing; all my life, I've on - ly been pre -

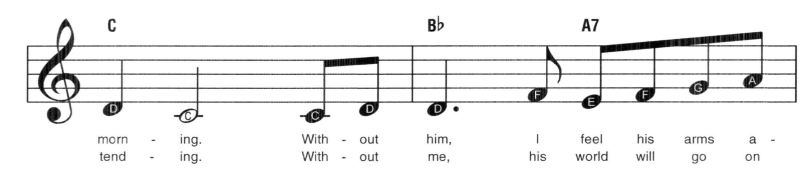

morn - ing. With - out him, I feel his arms a -
tend - ing. With - out me, his world will go on

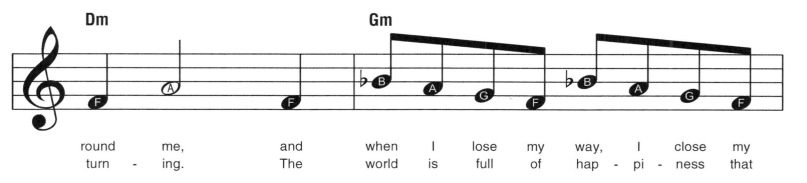

round me,   and   when   I   lose my   way, I   close my
turn - ing.   The   world is   full of   hap - pi - ness that

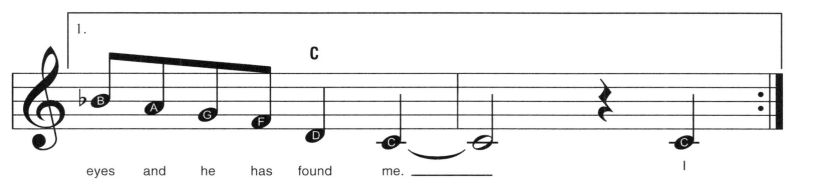

eyes   and   he   has   found   me. _____   I

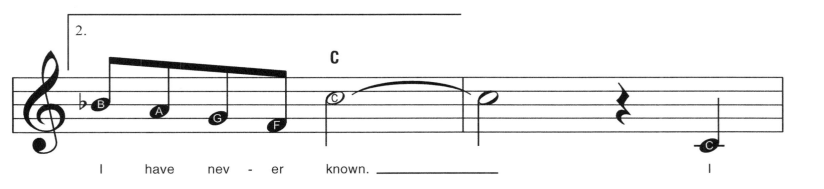

I   have   nev - er   known. _____   I

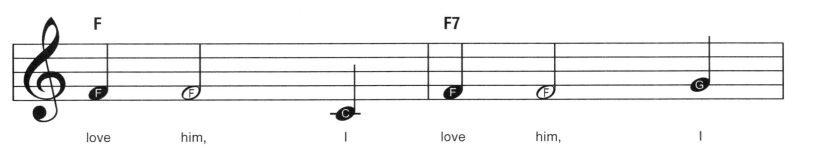

love   him,   I   love   him,   I

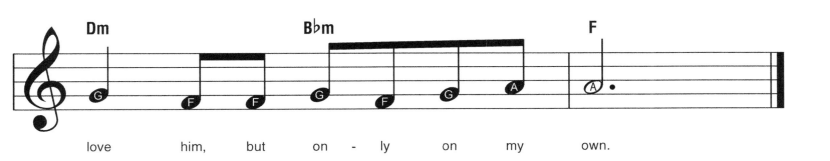

love   him,   but   on - ly   on   my   own.

Once Upon a Time
from the Broadway Musical ALL AMERICAN

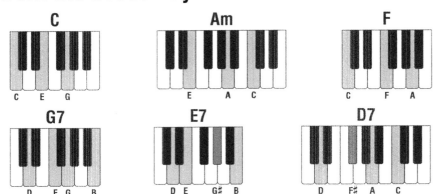

Lyric by Lee Adams
Music by Charles Strouse

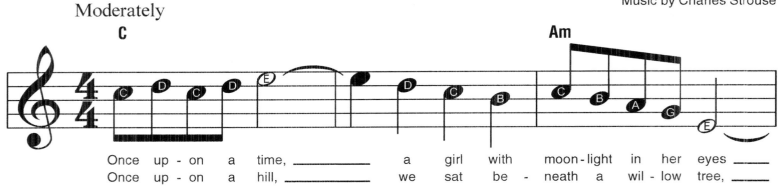

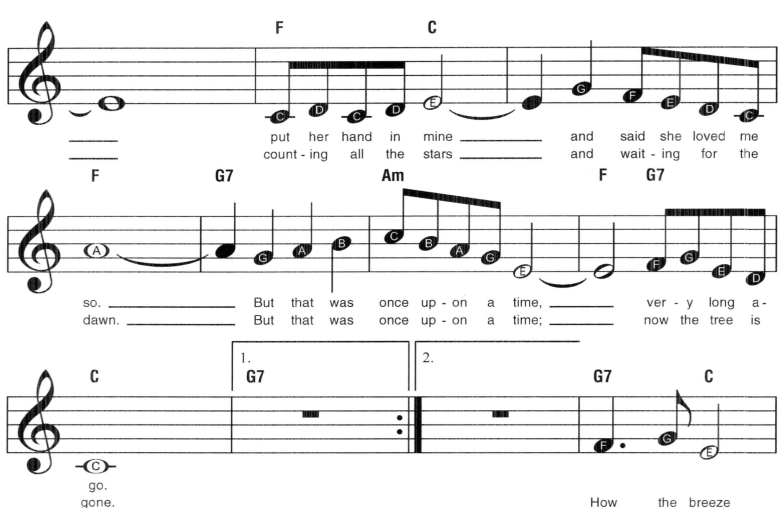

85

People

from FUNNY GIRL

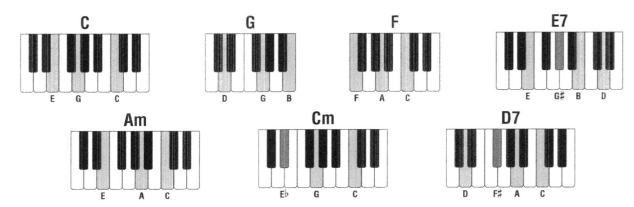

Words by Bob Merrill
Music by Jule Styne

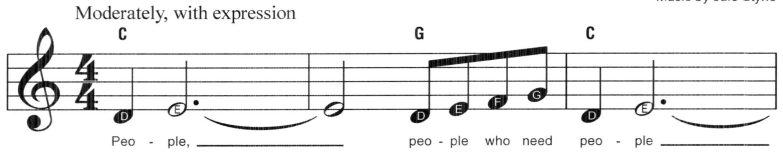

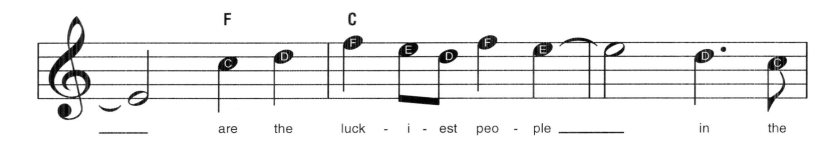

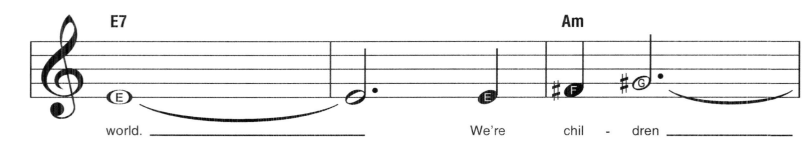

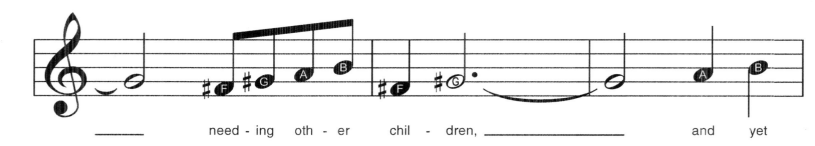

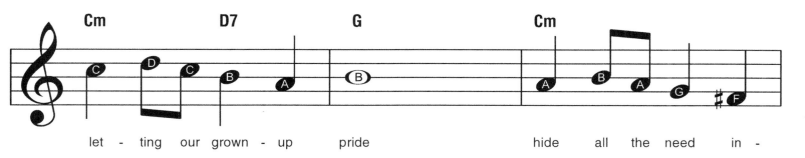

let - ting our grown - up pride hide all the need in -

side, act - ing more like chil - dren than

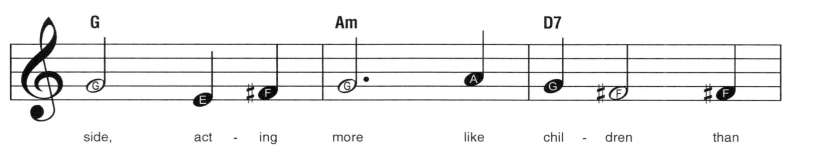

chil - dren. _____ Peo - ple, _____

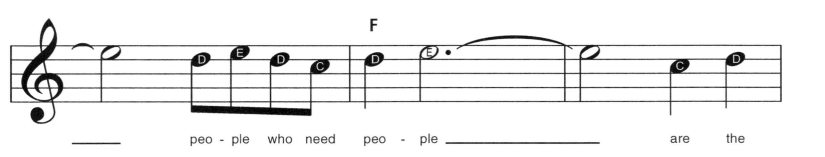

_____ peo - ple who need peo - ple _____ are the

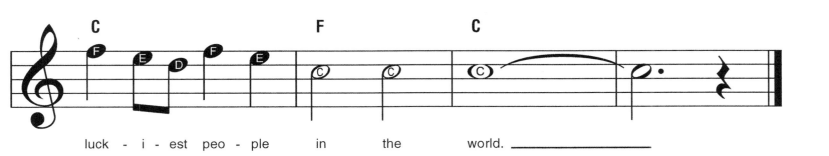

luck - i - est peo - ple in the world. _____

People Will Say We're in Love
from OKLAHOMA!

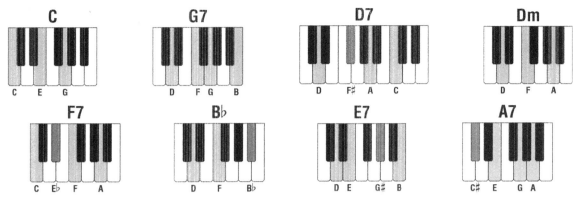

Lyrics by Oscar Hammerstein II
Music by Richard Rodgers

Put On a Happy Face
from BYE BYE BIRDIE

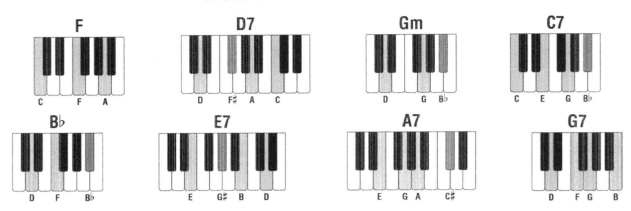

Lyric by Lee Adams
Music by Charles Strouse

Brightly

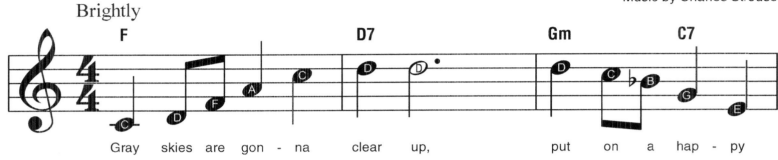

Gray skies are gon - na clear up, put on a hap - py

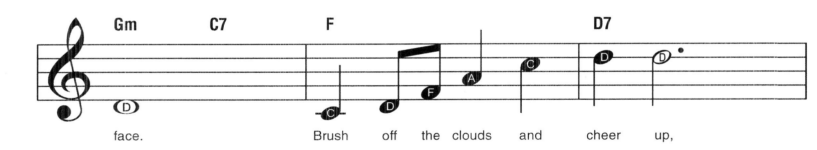

face. Brush off the clouds and cheer up,

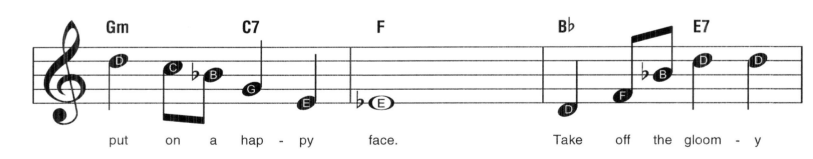

put on a hap - py face. Take off the gloom - y

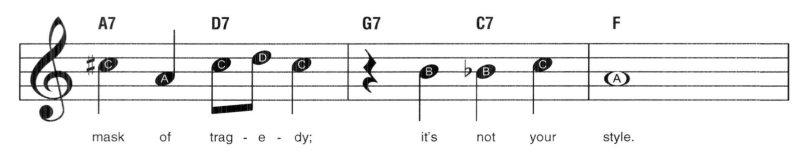

mask of trag - e - dy; it's not your style.

You'll look so good that you'll be glad you de - cid - ed to smile! __

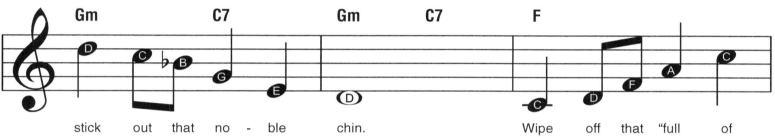

__ Pick out a pleas - ant out - look,

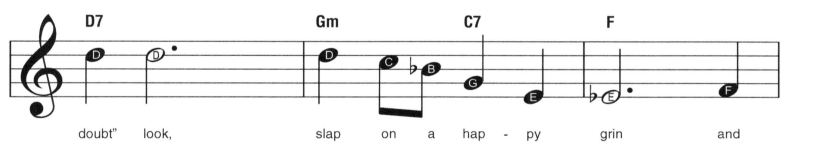

stick out that no - ble chin. Wipe off that "full of

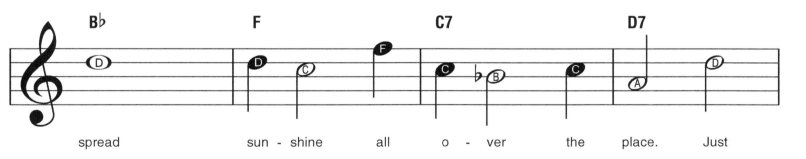

doubt" look, slap on a hap - py grin and

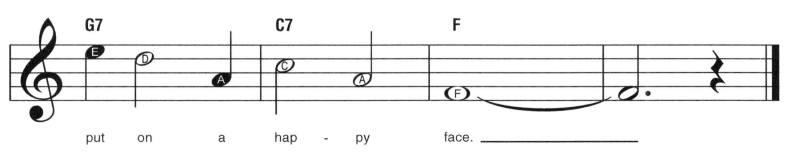

spread sun - shine all o - ver the place. Just

put on a hap - py face. ___

Puttin' On the Ritz
featured in YOUNG FRANKENSTEIN

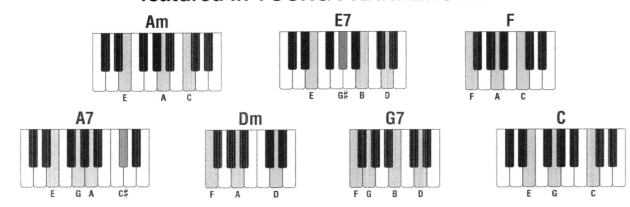

Words and Music by
Irving Berlin

Rhythmic Shuffle

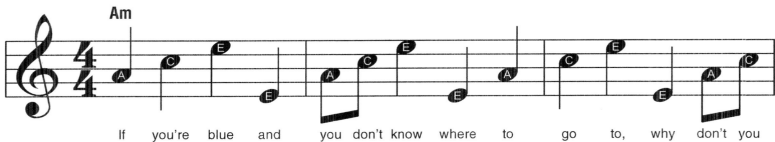

If you're blue and you don't know where to go to, why don't you

go where fash - ion sits, _____ put - tin' on the Ritz.

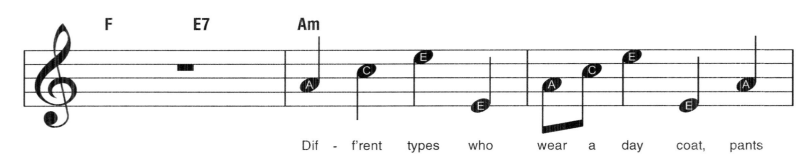

Dif - f'rent types who wear a day coat, pants

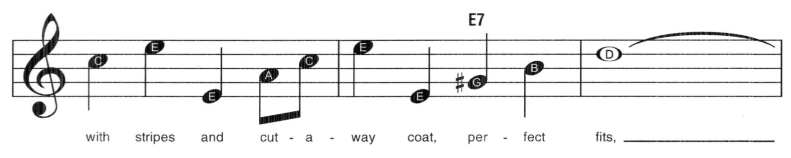

with stripes and cut - a - way coat, per - fect fits, _____

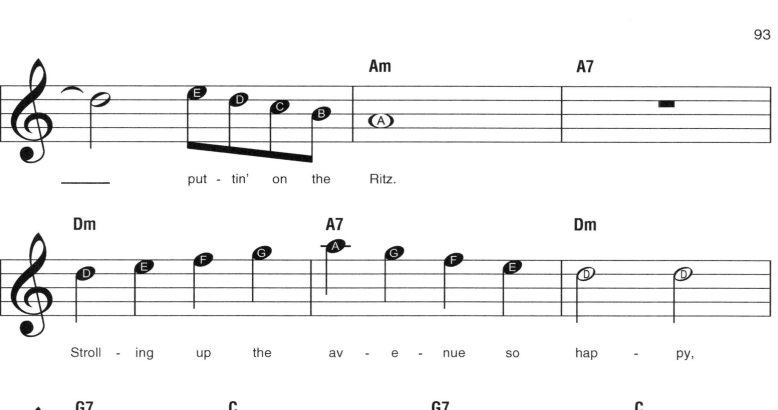

put - tin' on the Ritz.

Stroll - ing up the av - e - nue so hap - py,

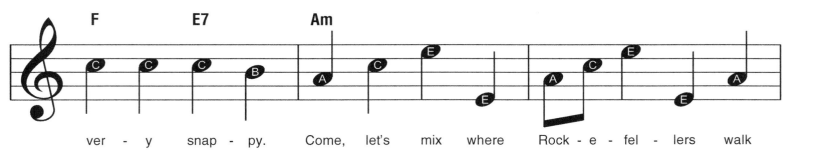

all dressed up just like an Eng - lish chap - pie,

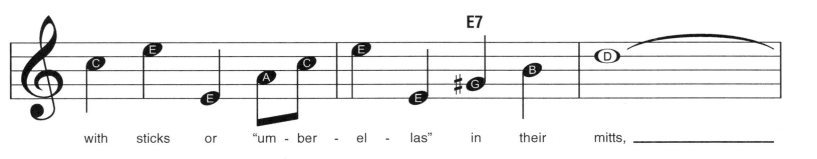

ver - y snap - py. Come, let's mix where Rock - e - fel - lers walk

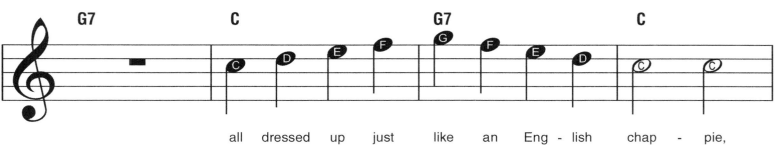

with sticks or "um - ber - el - las" in their mitts, _____

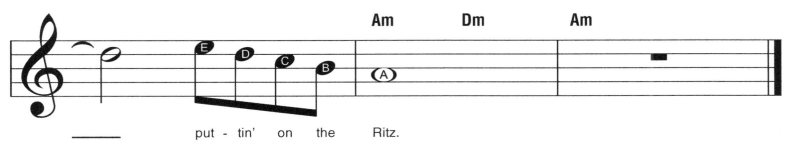

put - tin' on the Ritz.

'S Wonderful

from AN AMERICAN IN PARIS

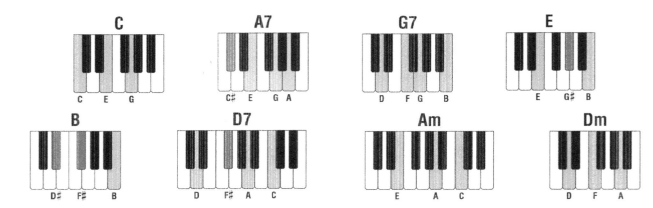

Music and Lyrics by George Gershwin
and Ira Gershwin

Easy Shuffle

'S won - der - ful, _____ 's mar - ve - lous _____

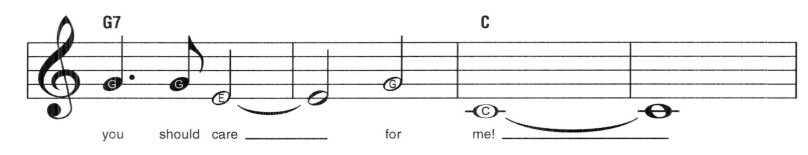

you should care _____ for me! _____

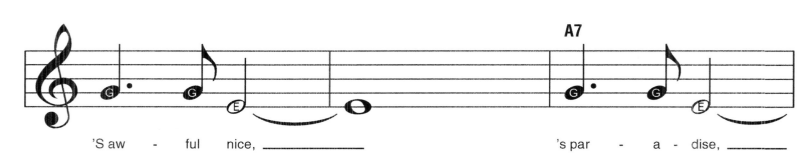

'S aw - ful nice, _____ 's par - a - dise, _____

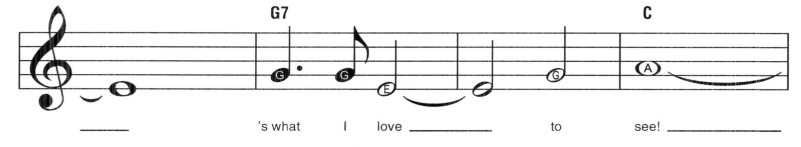

_____ 's what I love _____ to see! _____

95

Seasons of Love
from RENT

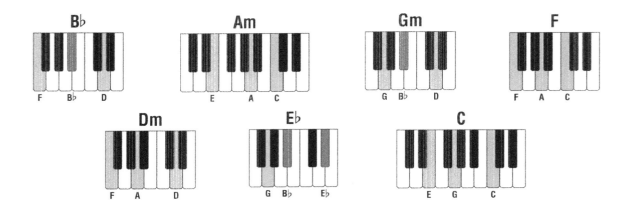

Words and Music by
Jonathan Larson

Moderately

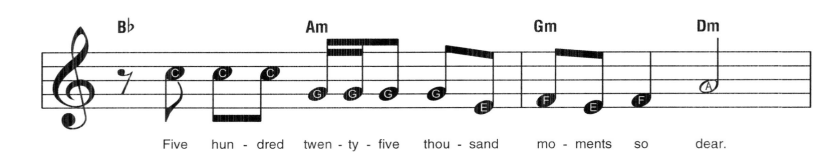

Five hun-dred twen-ty-five thou-sand six hun-dred min-utes.

Five hun-dred twen-ty-five thou-sand mo-ments so dear.

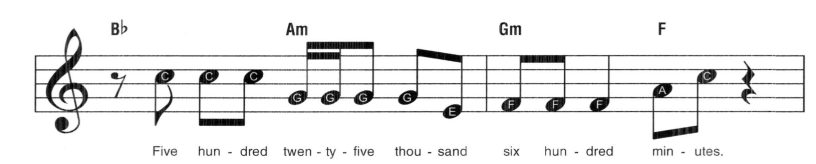

Five hun-dred twen-ty-five thou-sand six hun-dred min-utes.

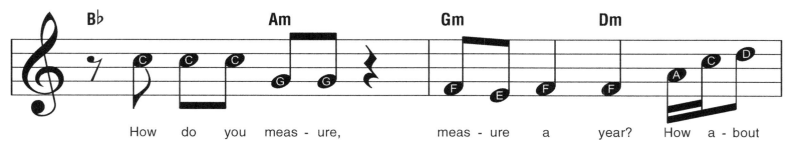

How do you meas - ure, meas - ure a year? How a - bout

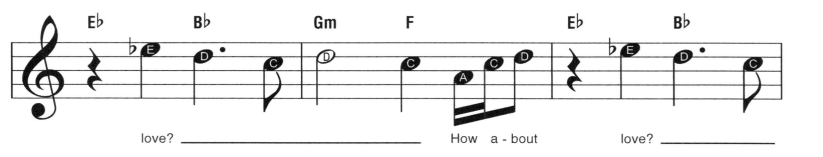

love? _____ How a - bout love? _____

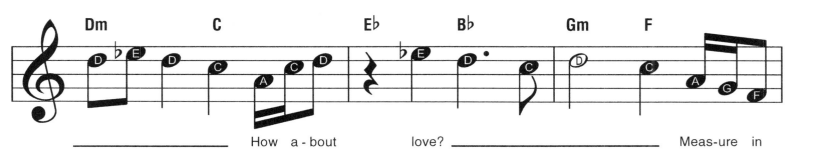

_____ How a - bout love? _____ Meas-ure in

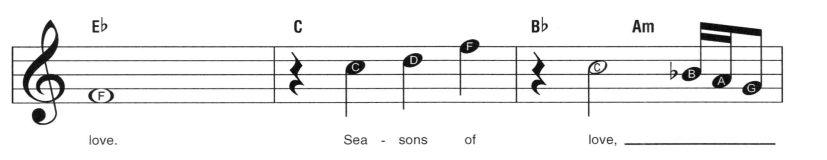

love. Sea - sons of love, _____

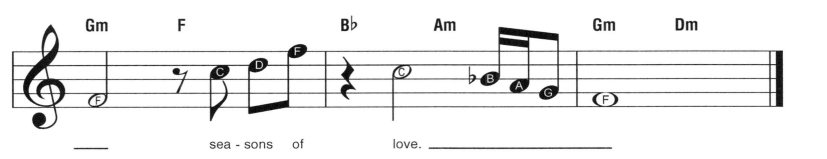

_____ sea - sons of love. _____

Send in the Clowns
from the Musical A LITTLE NIGHT MUSIC

Words and Music by
Stephen Sondheim

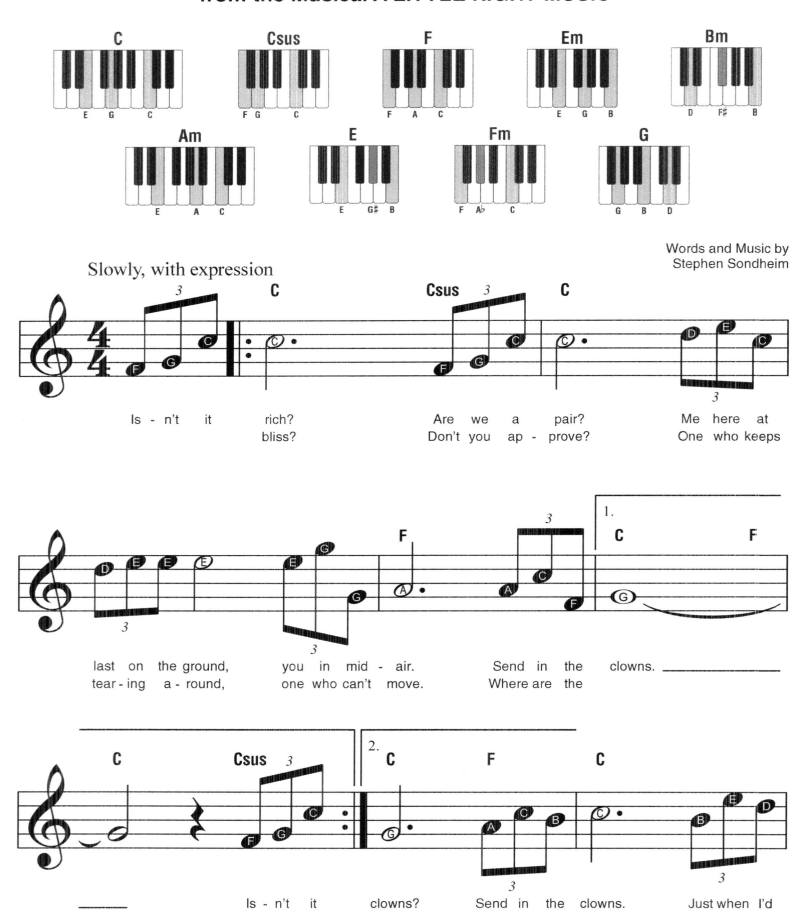

Singin' in the Rain

from SINGIN' IN THE RAIN

G   Em   D7

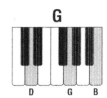
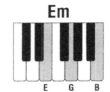
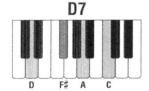

Lyric by Arthur Freed
Music by Nacio Herb Brown

Cheerful Shuffle

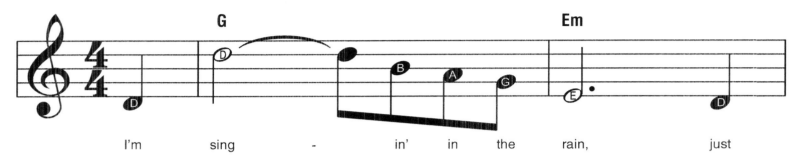

I'm sing - in' in the rain, just

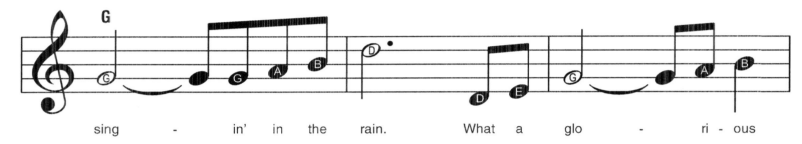

sing - in' in the rain. What a glo - ri - ous

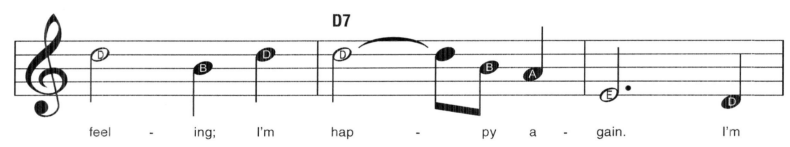

feel - ing; I'm hap - py a - gain. I'm

laugh - ing at clouds, so dark up a -

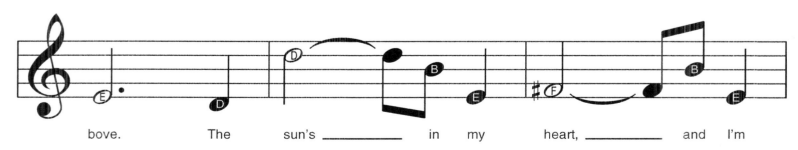

bove. The sun's _____ in my heart, _____ and I'm

Soliloquy
from CAROUSEL

Lyrics by Oscar Hammerstein II
Music by Richard Rodgers

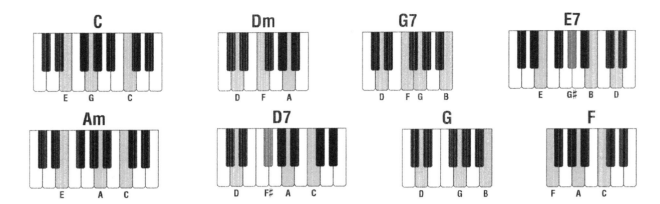

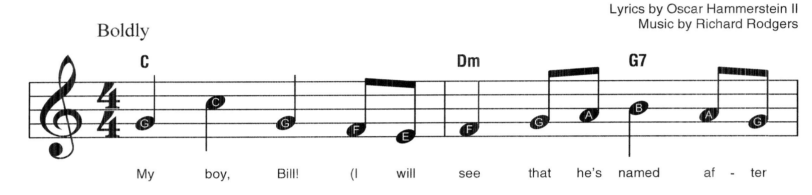

My boy, Bill! (I will see that he's named af - ter

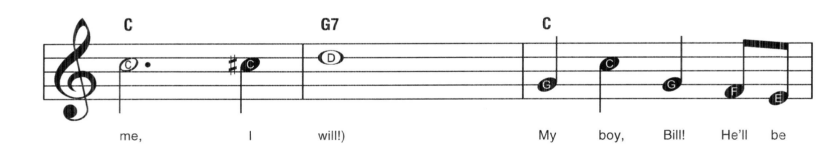

me, I will!) My boy, Bill! He'll be

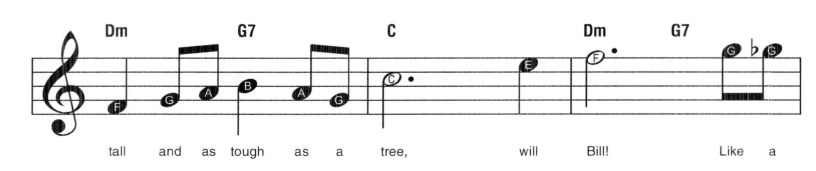

tall and as tough as a tree, will Bill! Like a

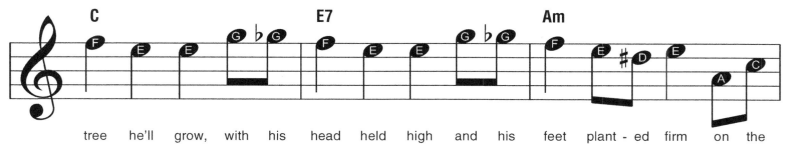

tree he'll grow, with his head held high and his feet plant-ed firm on the

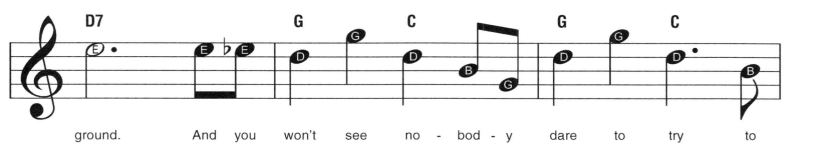

ground. And you won't see no-bod-y dare to try to

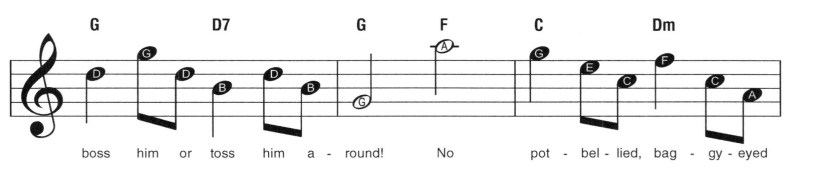

boss him or toss him a-round! No pot-bel-lied, bag-gy-eyed

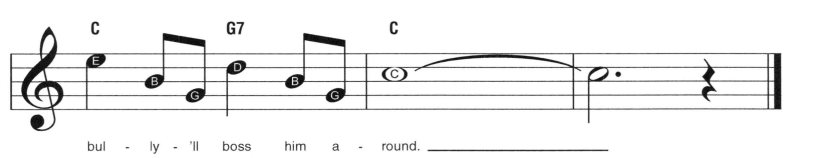

bul-ly-'ll boss him a-round. _____

Some Enchanted Evening

from SOUTH PACIFIC

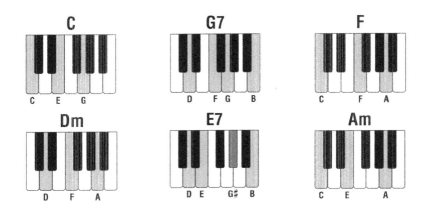

Lyrics by Oscar Hammerstein II
Music by Richard Rodgers

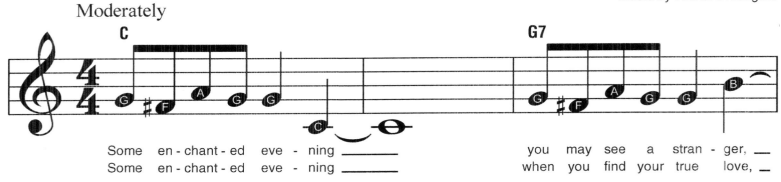

Some en-chant-ed eve - ning _____ you may see a stran - ger, ___
Some en-chant-ed eve - ning _____ when you find your true love, ___

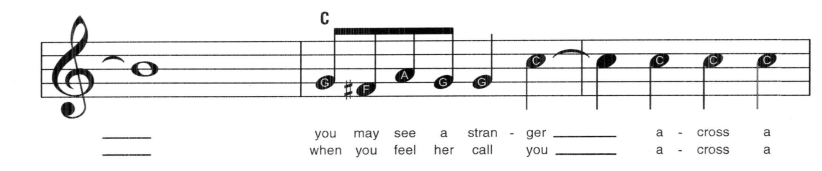

_____ you may see a stran - ger _____ a - cross a
_____ when you feel her call you _____ a - cross a

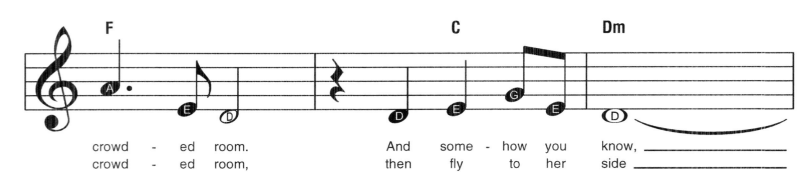

crowd - ed room. And some - how you know, _____
crowd - ed room, then fly to her side _____

Summer Nights

from GREASE

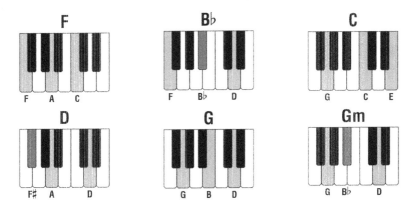

Lyric and Music by Warren Casey
and Jim Jacobs

'50s Pop feel

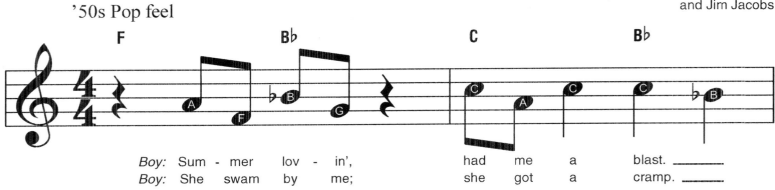

Boy: Sum - mer lov - in',   had me a blast. _____
Boy: She swam by me;   she got a cramp. _____

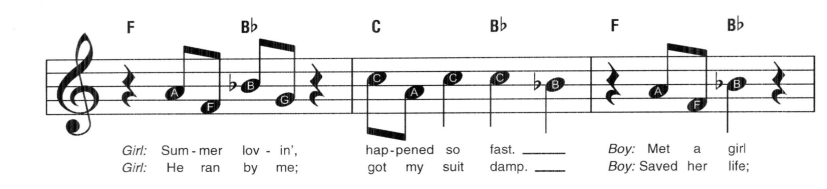

Girl: Sum - mer lov - in',   hap-pened so fast. _____   Boy: Met a girl
Girl: He ran by me;   got my suit damp. _____   Boy: Saved her life;

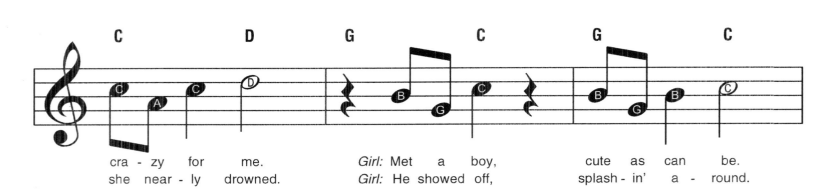

cra - zy for me.   Girl: Met a boy,   cute as can be.
she near - ly drowned. Girl: He showed off,   splash - in' a - round.

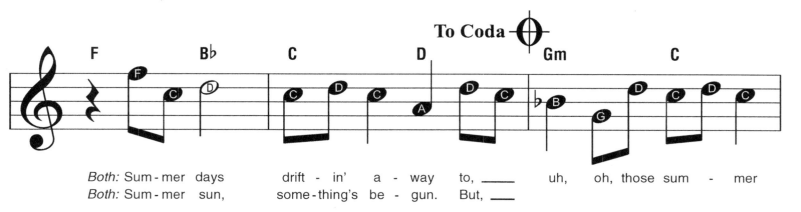

Both: Sum - mer days   drift - in' a - way to, ____ uh, oh, those sum - mer
Both: Sum - mer sun,   some - thing's be - gun. But, ___

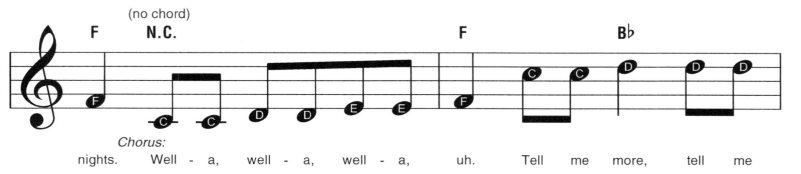

(no chord)

Chorus:
nights. Well - a, well - a, well - a, uh.   Tell   me   more,   tell   me

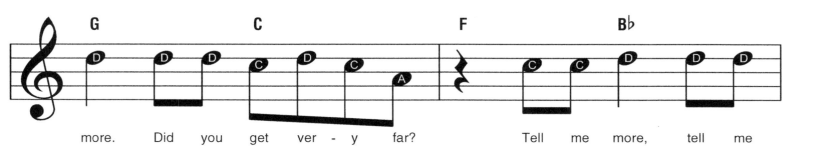

more. Did you get ver - y far?   Tell   me   more,   tell   me

D.C. al Coda
(Return to beginning,
play to ⊕ and skip to Coda)

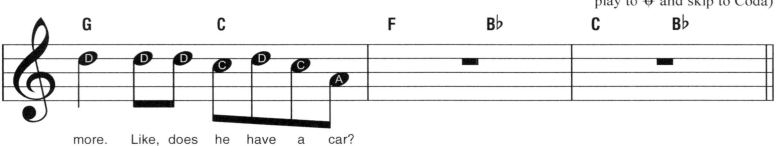

more. Like, does he have a car?

CODA

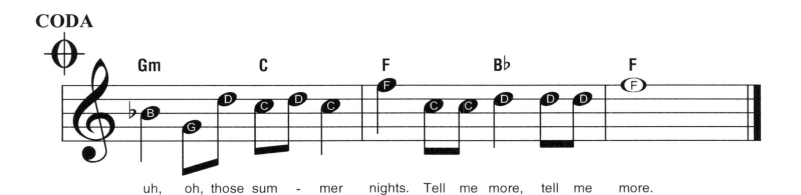

uh, oh, those sum - mer nights. Tell me more, tell me more.

Sunrise, Sunset
from the Musical FIDDLER ON THE ROOF

Words by Sheldon Harnick
Music by Jerry Bock

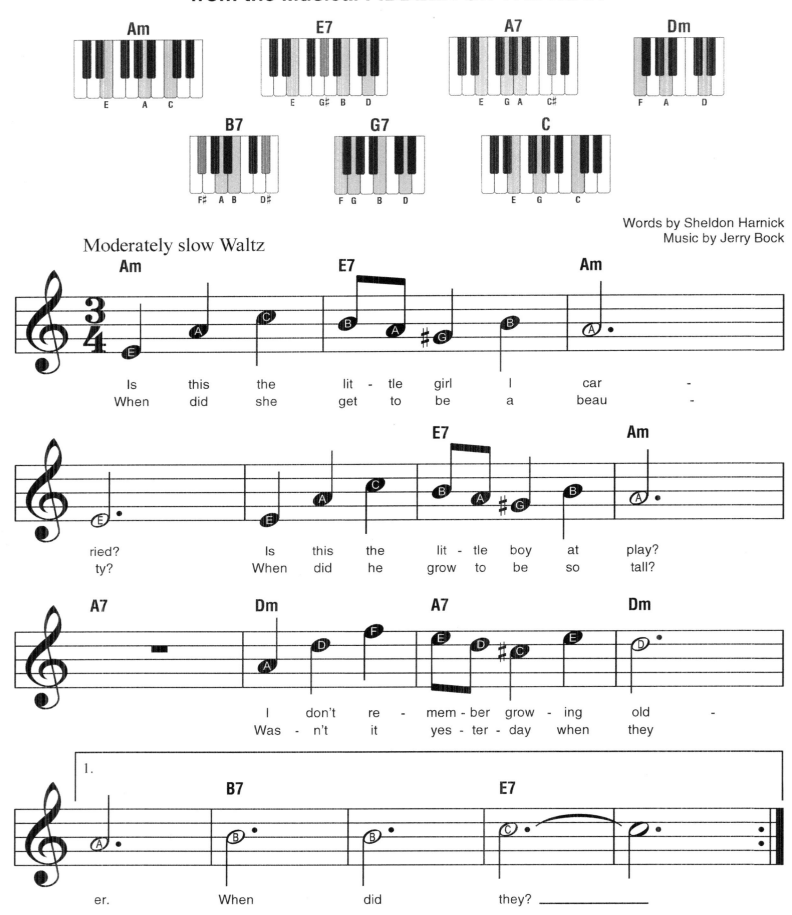

109

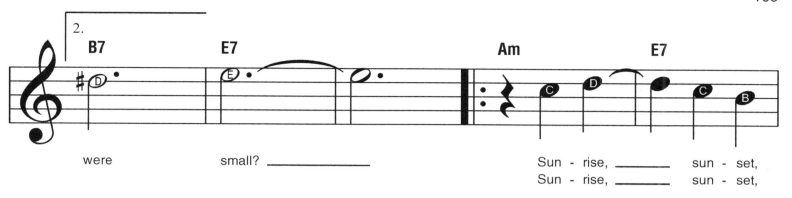

were   small? _____

Sun - rise, _____ sun - set,
Sun - rise, _____ sun - set,

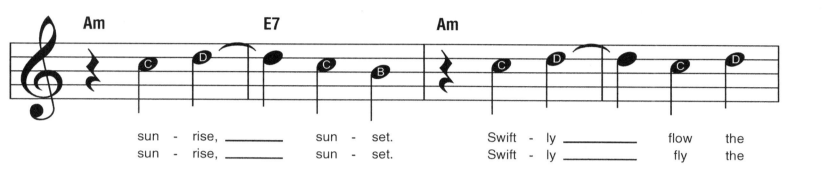

sun - rise, _____ sun - set.
sun - rise, _____ sun - set.

Swift - ly _____ flow the
Swift - ly _____ fly the

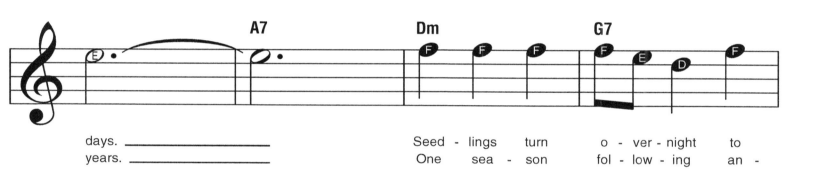

days. _____
years. _____

Seed - lings turn   o - ver - night   to
One sea - son   fol - low - ing   an -

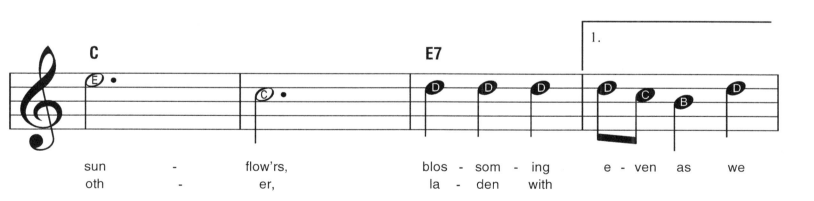

sun -   flow'rs,   blos - som - ing   e - ven as we
oth -   er,   la - den with

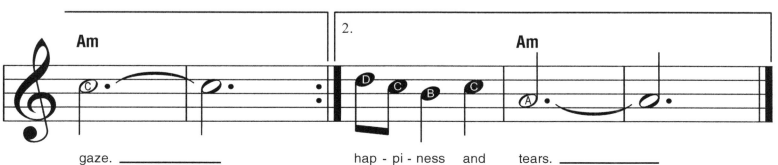

gaze. _____

hap - pi - ness and tears. _____

The Surrey with the Fringe on Top
from OKLAHOMA!

Lyrics by Oscar Hammerstein II
Music by Richard Rodgers

Cheerfully

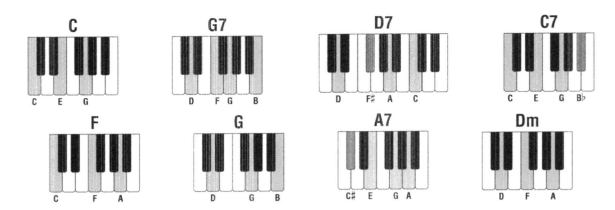

Chicks and ducks and geese bet - ter scur - ry   when I take you
Watch that fringe and see how it flut - ters   when I drive you

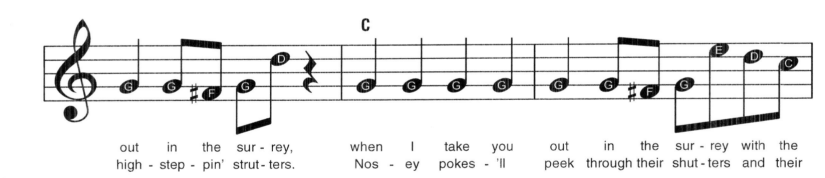

out in the sur - rey,   when I take you out in the sur - rey with the
high - step - pin' strut - ters.   Nos - ey pokes - 'll peek through their shut - ters and their

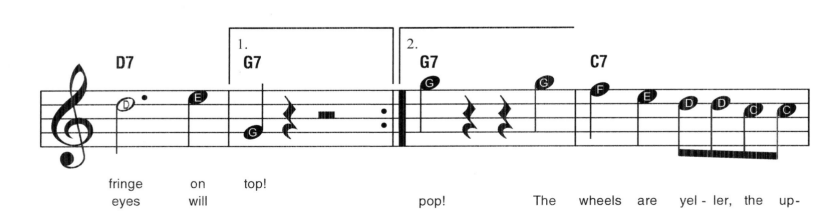

fringe on top!
eyes will   pop! The wheels are yel - ler, the up-

Thank Heaven for Little Girls

from GIGI

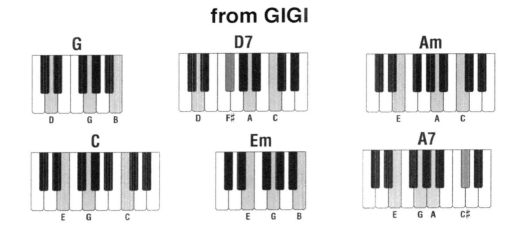

Words by Alan Jay Lerner
Music by Frederick Loewe

Moderately bright

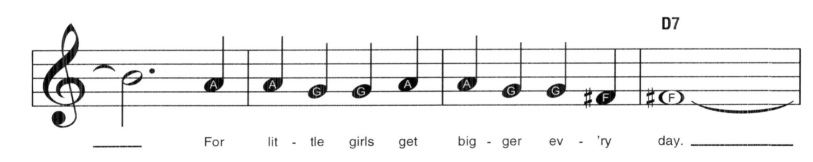

Thank heav - en _____ for lit - tle girls! _____

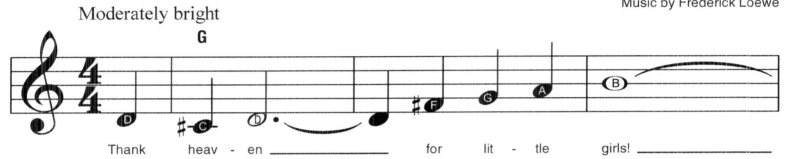

_____ For lit - tle girls get big - ger ev - 'ry day. _____

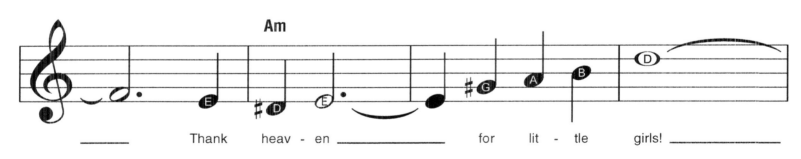

_____ Thank heav - en _____ for lit - tle girls! _____

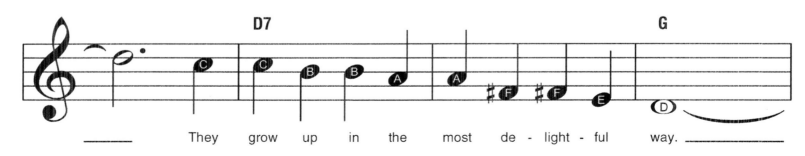

_____ They grow up in the most de - light - ful way. _____

Tonight
from WEST SIDE STORY

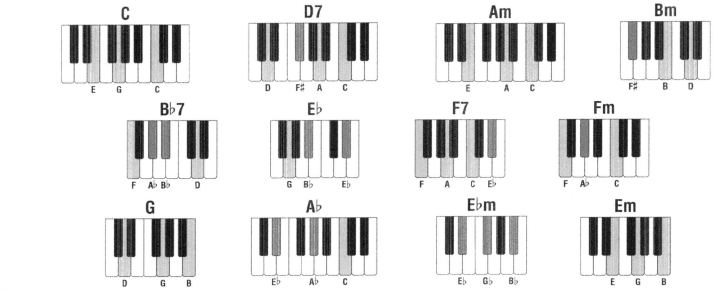

Lyrics by Stephen Sondheim
Music by Leonard Bernstein

Brightly

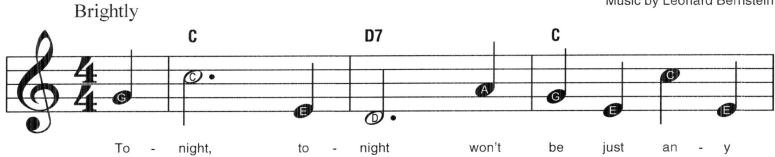

To - night, to - night won't be just an - y

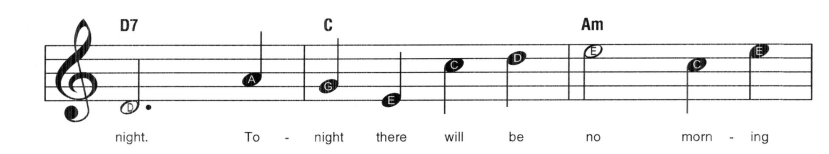

night. To - night there will be no morn - ing

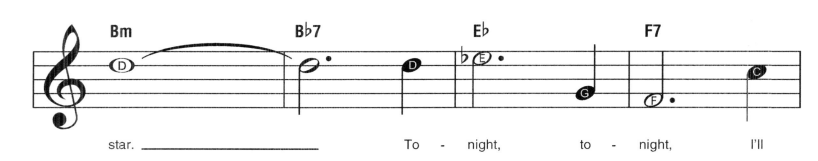

star. _____ To - night, to - night, I'll

Try to Remember
from THE FANTASTICKS

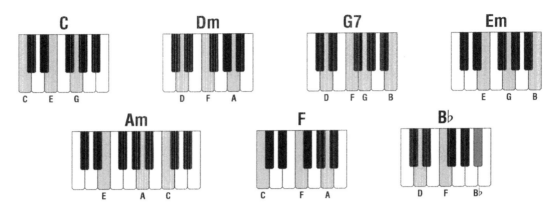

Words by Tom Jones
Music by Harvey Schmidt

Gentle Waltz

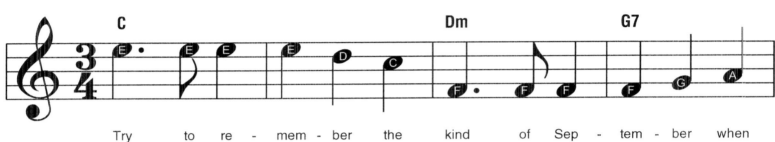

Try to re - mem - ber the kind of Sep - tem - ber when

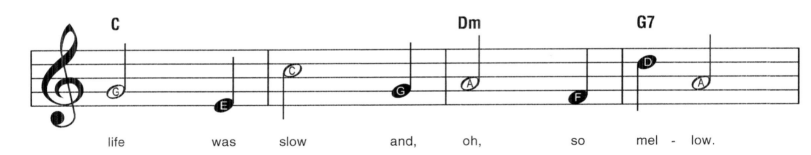

life was slow and, oh, so mel - low.

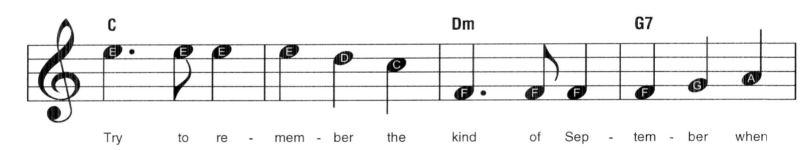

Try to re - mem - ber the kind of Sep - tem - ber when

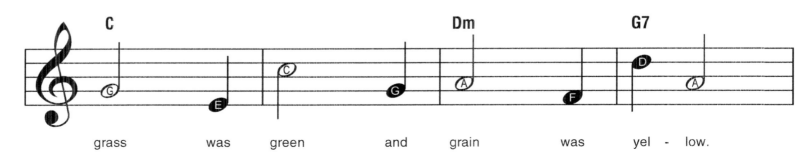

grass was green and grain was yel - low.

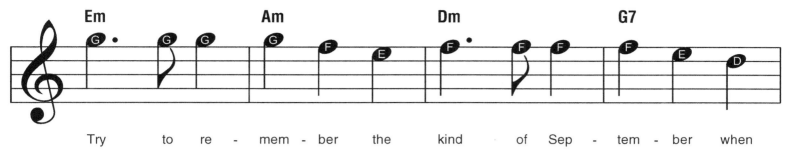

Try to re - mem - ber the kind of Sep - tem - ber when

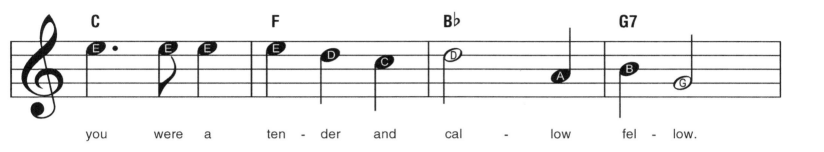

you were a ten - der and cal - low fel - low.

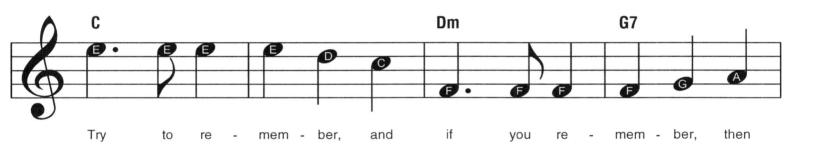

Try to re - mem - ber, and if you re - mem - ber, then

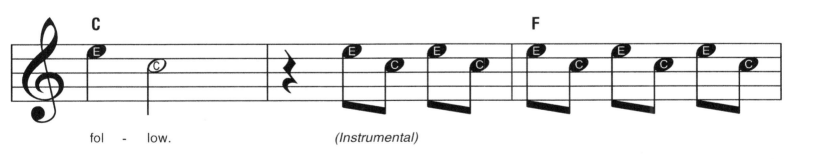

fol - low.   *(Instrumental)*

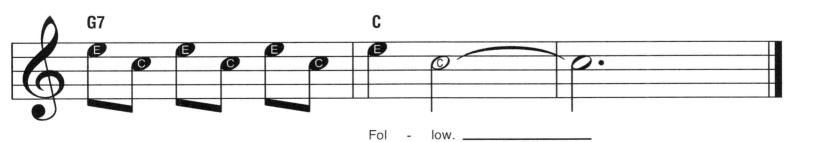

Fol - low. _____

You'll Never Walk Alone
from CAROUSEL

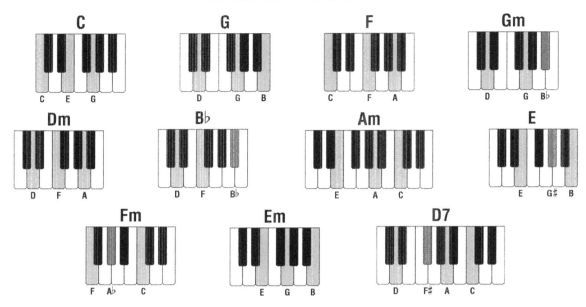

Lyrics by Oscar Hammerstein II
Music by Richard Rodgers

Moderately

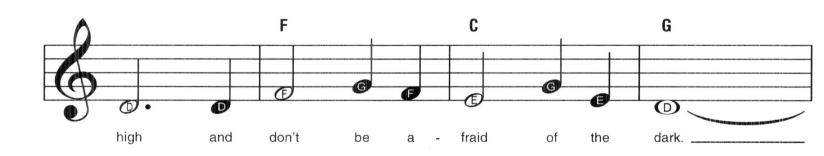

When you walk through a storm, hold your head up

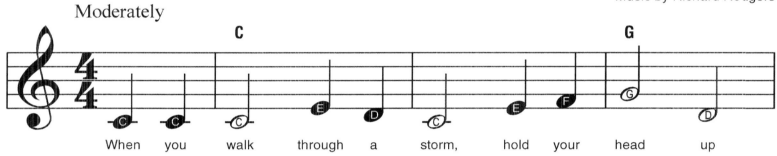

high and don't be a - fraid of the dark. _____

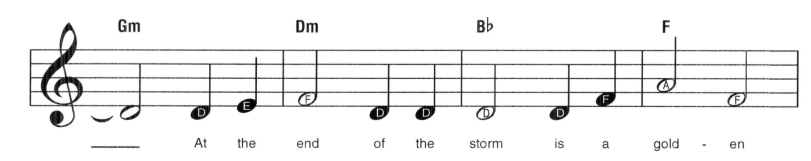

_____ At the end of the storm is a gold - en

Summertime
from PORGY AND BESS®

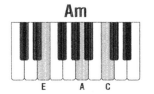
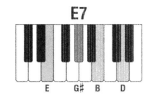

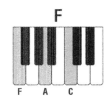
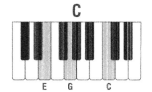

Music and Lyrics by George Gershwin,
DuBose and Dorothy Heyward
and Ira Gershwin

Lazy Shuffle

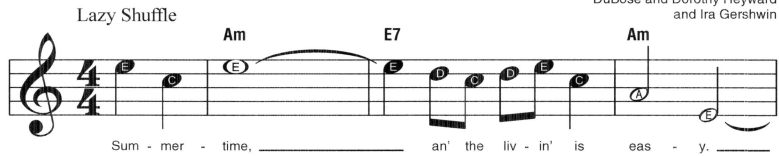

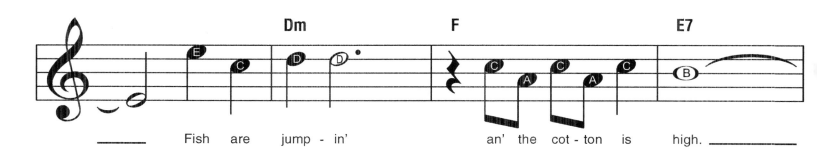

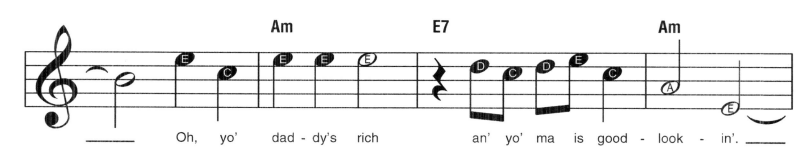

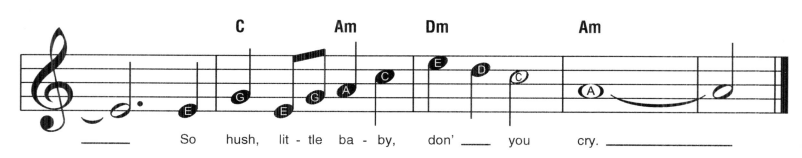